Who Are You?

by

Russell Wetherington

Request additional copies
from Amazon.com
or contact the author at whoareyou-rwetherington,com

ISBN 978-1-57550-070-6

Printed in the United States of America

Cover Art by Johanna M. Bolton
April 2016

10   9   8   7   6   5   4   3   2   1

DEDICATION

This book, Who Are You?
is dedicated to my mother,

Anna Belle Kersey Wetherington,

who raised five boys as a single mom,
and kept us all together
through the bad times and good times;

and to my brothers,
Jack, Clifford, George, and Wayne;

and my son and daughter,
Steven and Crystal;

and my best friend and wife, Michele,
who has encouraged me throughout this time
while writing the book.

TABLE OF CONTENTS

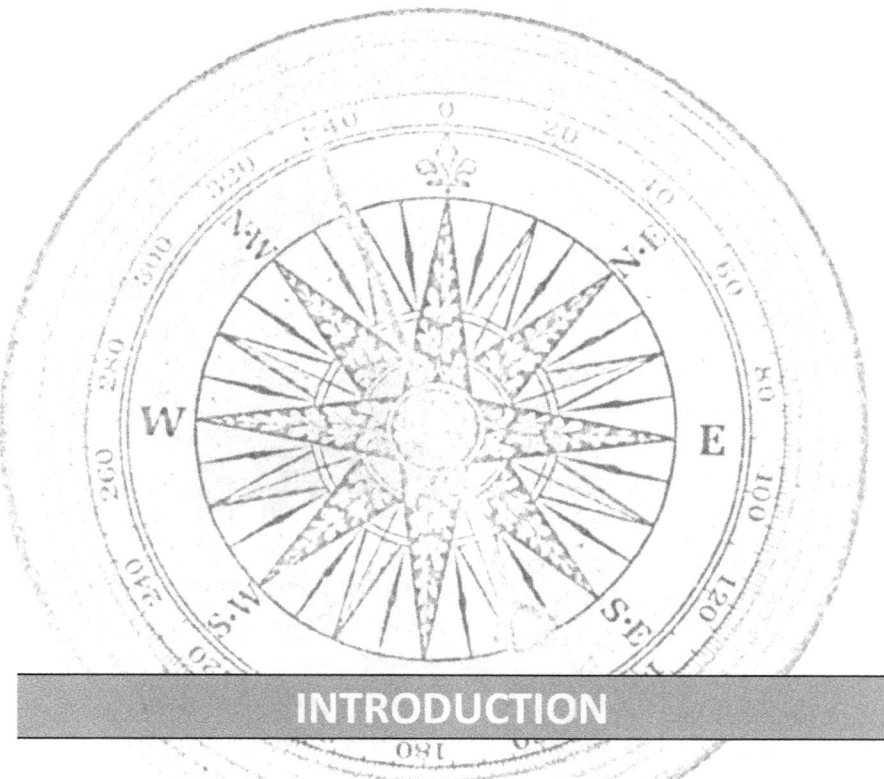

INTRODUCTION

WHO ARE YOU? was written for *you*. And why do I say you? I want to share with you how a kid from a poor family can make it and overcome many obstacles and be successful. Also, it is designed for a special group of people – busy people. Are you a busy person? Are you someone who works all day and then hurries home in order to spend time with your children at a practice or game they may be playing? Then after dinner and bedtime are you thinking about what you have to do at work the next day?

I will be sharing some life experiences with you and I hope they will help you better your life in some little way. Growing up I was the middle child of five boys. Yes, five boys. We did not have a lot growing up, but our mother kept the five of us together by working hard and providing food on our table.

We lived in the housing projects when I was in elementary school, and that was an experience to say the least. I remember many times going outside to play all day long and then play hide and seek at night. One night while playing hide and seek and using a truck as home base I came in running to home free, but I ran into the back of the truck which had a big trailer hitch and I sliced my left thigh wide open. It took over 100 stitches inside and out to sew it up. The doctors were not sure how much I would be able to use my leg

My Mom, me, & my brothers, all dressed up for Easter Sunday service, 1960. From left to right: front — me, Wayne, George; back — Jack, Mom, Cliff.

later. I was determined to not only use my leg, but fully use it to play football and baseball which I was able to do. That was the first lesson I learned that if you are determined anything is possible.

I started working at a very early age and worked throughout high school, and I also played sports. I was able to purchase a new car when I was a senior in high school because I worked hard and saved my money.

I enlisted in the Air Force only six months after graduating from high school, because I did not know what I wanted to do with my life. I started taking college courses at night, but it was difficult to see the light at the end of the tunnel. So, in 1976 I applied for Educational discharge to enter into a two-year Air Force Reserve Officers Training Corp. (AFROTC) program at the University of Nebraska at Omaha to get my degree and my commission as an officer in the Air Force. The only problem was that I had to complete three years of college in two years. Not only was I able to get my degree in two years, but I graduated as a Distinguished AFROTC graduate.

I was asked by a friend of mine, after I went back on active duty in the Air Force, if I read the Bible. At the time I had to answer no, I do not have time. He suggested that I start by reading Proverbs because Proverbs has 31 chapters and it would only take three to five minutes to read one chapter a day. I started reading chapter one of Proverbs on the first day of the month, followed by chapter two on the second day, and continued until I read all 31 chapters during the month of July. I was surprised that it only took me three to five minutes each day, and I was amazed at the wisdom that popped out at me when I read the chapter.

It is not surprising that you can read the same passage of scripture and get a different message each time you read it, but it is more amazing when you read 15 minutes a day and how your life will become better in some way.

I have set this book up in 31 chapters or days. It is set up for you to read one chapter each day of the month (i.e. if today is July 1 you read Day One) and use this as a guide to improve your life. It will be amazing when you read it and when you read it again the following month. Every time you read the chapter something different is going to jump out at you, and you will take notice and say to yourself this is what I needed to hear today. I developed an associated journal for you to record what you learn from each daily reading.

WHO ARE YOU? was written for people who say they do not have fifteen minutes a day to read, to work on improving themselves through the daily readings. I invite you to make fifteen minutes available everyday morning or night to read and learn. This book is set up so you can read a chapter a day for each day of the month.

The greatest pleasure in life is doing what people say you can't do! Quote by Albert Einstein really sums up my book. *"I must be willing to give up what I am, in order to become what I will be."*

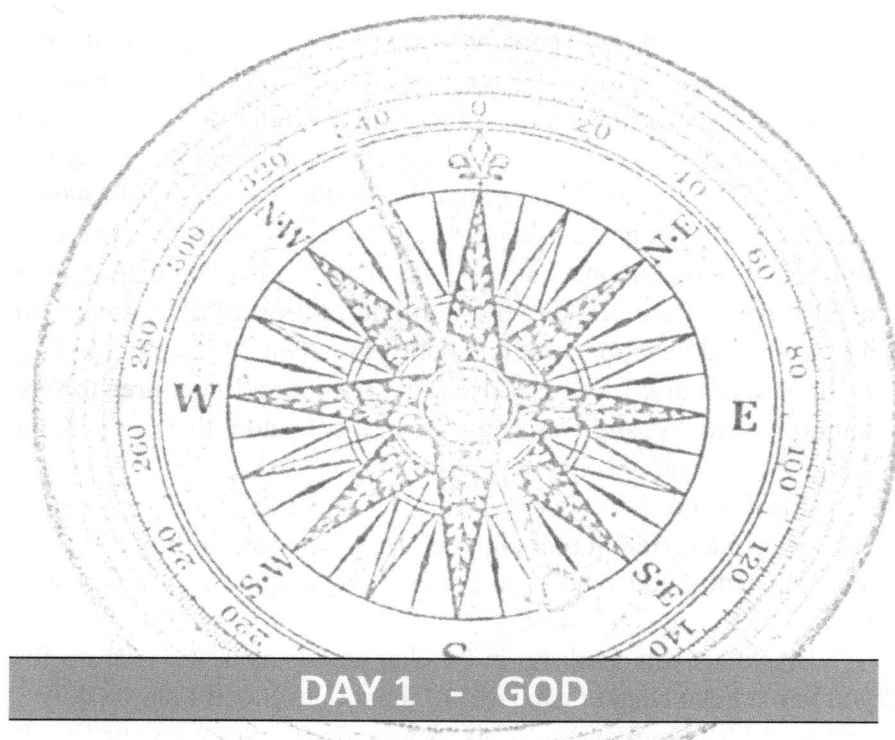

DAY 1   -   GOD

*Matthew 6:33 - Seek first the kingdom of God and his right-eousness, and all these things shall be
added to you.*

Jeremiah 29:1 – "I know the plans I have for you; declares the Lord, plans to prosper you and not to harm you, plans to give you hope and a future." All of what we are both good and bad is what we have thought and believed. What you've become is the price you paid to get what you used to want.

Wondering what God has planned for you? We simply need to open our hearts to him, listen, and wait. Today will never occur again.

"I know God will not give me anything I can't handle; I just wish he didn't trust me so much." Mother Teresa

Our nation was founded under the principles of God on our money it reads "In God We Trust." Please be patient. God isn't finished with me yet. What it really means is that there is always room for improvement.

Troubles, problems, or situations compel you to re-evaluate your life and priorities. Are you taking God seriously? Have you surrendered yourself to him or do you struggle against his will? Do you look forward to prayer as an intimate time of sharing with the Father or has it become empty? Are you on the right path in your spiritual journey or has the road you have chosen taken you away from God and his purpose for your life? Change the direction in which you are looking for happiness. So often we can get ourselves into what grandma used to call "pickles" or "pickle jams." We look back on times we did dumb things or even wrong things. I remember one time I ran away from home because I got suspended from school for gambling. I did not want to face my mom. I felt I had let her down and she would be disappointed in me. There is a saying "Wisdom is when you experience something." You grow in wisdom.

There is no way you or I or anyone else for that matter knows what the future holds. I think, if you knew what God had planned for you, you would take every detour to avoid traveling the road map that God has planned for you.

I remember one time I mentioned to my wife, Michele, that she was not #1 but God was #1. The only way I could honor and respect Michele as my wife was to have God as #1 in my life.

The way I look at the priority list is in this order:

God
Spouse
Family
Job

God never assigns a job without providing the tools to accomplish it. Be a blessing to someone. You have a blessing inside that someone needs to hear. Be good to people!

You did it again. You let someone's opinion of you affect you. The truth is that it doesn't matter what others may think of us. You don't work for your boss's praise or your wife's or children's. We strive to do all that we do to honor God. God is the only one that matters. Live in such a way that those who know you but don't know God will come to know God because they know you.

Yes, I am a Christian, but I am not trying to convert you or preach to you, but only let you know where I stand. For some of you who don't believe that God exists, I would like to share a story.

Once upon a time there was a little boy who had been going to Sunday School for a few years. After hearing about God for so long he decided it was time to go look for God himself. He thought the journey might be long, so he found an old gym bag that was his father's; he stocked up on root beer, granola bars, and Snackwells and then he set off without telling his mother he was going. He was about seven years old. Well, he hadn't gotten very far when he got tired and decided to rest a while.

There was a park nearby, so he cut across the grass to a bench. There was only one other person in the park, an old, old woman who was sitting on the bench. He climbed up beside her. The two sat there and didn't say anything for the longest time. Then he turned to her and asked her if she was thirsty. She smiled at him and nodded. Out came the root beer. They shared and sat in silence. Then they ate the cookies and granola bars and finished the root beer. They were together about an hour and she didn't say anything at all, just smiled at him every once in a while. So, he talked as little boys do. He told her stories of his mom and dad, brothers and sisters, first year at school, his pets, and everything he could think of.

Time passed and he thought of his mother at home. He realized that she'd be furious at him for going off without telling her, so he decided he had better go home. He got down from the bench and picked up his empty bag. They had finished everything. He said goodbye to the old woman and turned to go away. He took a few steps and stopped. He thought to himself, she has such a lovely smile! I want to see it again. So, he turned around and gave her a big hug and kiss. Her face broke out into that magnificent smile. He smiled back and headed for home.

His mother was waiting for him at the door, frantic. She grabbed hold of him and shook him. "Where were you? I told you never to go off without telling me. Where have you been? I have been worried sick."

He looked at her and smiled broadly. "You didn't have to worry. I spent the afternoon in the park with God!" Momentarily stunned his mother was speechless. He continued thoughtfully. "You know, I never thought she'd be so old and so quiet… and thirsty."

> God never assigns a job without providing the tools to accomplish it.

Meanwhile, the old woman had gotten up very slowly from her bench, picked up her cane and headed for home. Her son, about forty-five years old, was waiting for her, frantic. "Mother, he said. "How many times do I have to tell you not to go off on your own without telling me? I've been looking for you everywhere and was just about to call the paramedics and police again. You can't just go wandering off. Where have you been?"

Her face was radiant. She smiled at him and said "Oh, you needn't have worried. I spent the afternoon in the park with God."

Her son was stunned and thought to himself, "Oh dear, she's much worse than before." But she continued rather thoughtfully, "You know, I didn't expect him to be so young and so talkative… and he loves root beer, too!"

Everyone laughs of course when they hear the end of the story. It's almost too cute and yet both the boy and the old woman are onto something theological and true – the great and holy one of God's is in our midst.

Coincidence or chance! God knows what he is doing.

When we do what we can, God will do what we can't.

Now take 5 minutes and read Proverbs 1.

Don't read another chapter until you write one thing you have
learned from your readings today that will help you become a better person.

_____

_____

_____

_____

_____

_____

_____

_____

_____

_____

_____

_____

_____

_____

_____

_____

_____

*Proverbs 1:2 - That people may know wisdom and
  discipline.*

DAY 2 - ATTITUDE

Philippians 2:14-15 - Do all things without complaining and disputing, that you may become blameless and harmless, children of God without fault in the midst of a crooked and perverse generation, among whom you shine as lights in the world.

"Ability is what you're capable of doing. Motivation determines what you do. Attitude determines how well you do it."
Lou Holtz – Notre Dame Football Coach

Hardly a day passes without the word "attitude" entering a conversation at work or home. It may be used as a complaint or compliment. It could mean the difference between a promotion or a demotion. Your attitude is an inward feeling expressed by behavior. That is why your attitude can be seen a distance away without a word being said. Haven't we all noticed the pout of the sulkier, or the jutted jaw of the determined, or what we call in our family the "Annabelle (my mom) look?" Since an attitude often is expressed by our body language and by the looks on our faces, it can be contagious.

Have you noticed what happens to a group of people when one person by his/her expression reveals a negative attitude or the look of disapproval? Sometimes the attitude can be masked outwardly and others who see us are fooled. But, usually the cover up will not last long. There is that constant struggle as the attitude tries to wiggle its way out.

Attitude determines your altitude; a strong positive and resilient attitude will elevate you to unimaginable heights. In my opinion, in life, attitude is everything. Monday morning attitude – I was always asked "Why are you so happy on Monday?" I had to explain that I treat every workday as a Friday. Have you ever noticed how everyone gets happier as they get closer to Friday? That is why for many years I have taken the attitude to treat every weekday as a Friday and this really makes me feel good but throws everyone else off.

Change your attitude, change your life!

Change your attitude – change your life. You can do anything if you put your mind to it. Your attitude towards doing things is the only holdback. It's not your life that changes from moment to moment, it's your mood. Think about the previous statement for a minute. It's not your life that changes from moment top moment, it's your mood.

"A happy person is not a person in a certain set of circumstances, but rather a person with a certain set of attitudes."
Hugh Downs

Happiness starts with you! This is an inside job. It's all in the way you look at things. Think about it for a minute, when you look at something in a picture or better yet when you look at the nighttime sky. What do you see? One person is going to see the stars and the other person may see the moon first. The person looking at the moon, questions did the United States, Astronaut Neil Armstrong really walk on the moon. The person looking at the stars believes that each star is a miracle. Being happy is actually more a choice then a chance. Being happy seems to start developing during your childhood. You develop your attitude or mindsets from the people you are associated with; parents, grandparents, friends, classmates, coworkers and teachers. However, I truly believe you can change your mindset and be a happy and **a** positive person with a great attitude. This will not happen overnight but through reading good motivational books and being associated with the right people, you are on your way to enjoy the journey to discover your true happiness.

Our surroundings control our forming. Unquestionably, our surroundings help construct our attitudes. In our early years, our attitudes are determined mainly by our conditions in our surroundings.

To be humble is to accept that you are full of pride.

Totally yours – If you ever have an opportunity to keep your mouth shut, don't pass it up, we all can learn more by listening.

Sad – Do you get sad when you lose someone (family, friend or pet)? Being sad is normal sometimes. It's okay to allow yourself to be sad for a while.

Grateful – growing up was hard in our family; we didn't have a lot and sometimes we depended on other people to help. I was grateful and thankful to have something to eat sometimes. Growing up in Bunnell and St. Augustine, Florida we could always find potatoes and fruit. Hastings, Florida was one of the biggest producers of potatoes in the southeast, and there would be times we had a 50 lb. bag of potatoes given to us. I remember a lot of times making French fried potato sandwiches with mayonnaise on them. That would be dinner for us.

> Our attitudes are formed by our experiences and how we choose to react to them.

Also, back in the late 50's and 60's soda bottles were glass, and you received 1 cent to 3 cents for returning the bottles, so I would go along the side of the road picking up bottles that people had thrown away. I was very grateful for the little money I received for the bottles.

Doctor Mike O'Connor (my chiropractor) writes articles for his newsletter, and I would like to share an article he wrote about being grateful. Doctor Mike took a trip to Italy in 2015, and this is what he wrote upon his return:

"We had this lovely rooftop patio that overlooked the ancient city of Riva Del Garda (In Trentino). We got to know a lot of the local shopkeepers and bar owner's right underneath or on the tiny cobbled side streets just around the corner. Almost daily we would go down for an *apperativo* before dinner or for a shot of expresso in the morning before a hike or mountain climb. We would chat with the people there or with the baristas and get an insight as to what they thought about life and living. We love doing that! One can learn so much by asking a question and then shutting up and listening. I'm telling you this to make you proud and to appreciate something... your amazing and totally unique country! Virtually everyone there has such respect and admiration for the US of A! And well, they should! I don't even need to tell you the why.

They are grateful too. Think about Europe in the early 20th century and America's influence. I don't even need to tell you why. They shake their heads in awe when I tell them that we live on the east coast of Florida. Most of these seemingly simple folks have traveled extensively. They've been to Florida and adore it. They've seen the vast array of luxuries that we all take for granted. I don't even need to tell you what! We are blessed people in a blessed land. We have NO apologies to make. Despite that calming, provincial view from the top of that little Riva apartment. I'm happy and honored to be back in MY COUNTRY. There's nowhere...despite what shortsighted, complaining, entitlement mentality people or political groups say, like this great land of ours. And, by the way, according to scores that I talked with, WE THE PEOPLE, yes, you and I, are a wonderful, unique breed too! They look at us as giving, highly adventurous and courageous people... Americans... innovative and strong.

I believe that, too. We all should. Sometimes we need to step out of the everyday bustle of our daily lives and routines to see it. WE ALL need to get away. I don't even need to tell you why! I'm going to leave you with this. Do you know what neuroscientists have pinpointed as the emotion of healing and health in the human body? If you guessed happiness, you're wrong. Being happy is a symptom - a good symptom of living correctly and thinking correctly.

The answer is GRATITUDE. Being grateful builds new cells faster, charges the mitochondria and emits bio-chemicals from our glands that reduce stress and reinforce immunity.

Gratefulness also leads to that elusive, ethereal emotion, happiness. The dude on the beer commercial says, "Stay hungry, my friend." I say. Be grateful. I sure am."

Dr. Mike O'Connor

Happiness is something you decide on ahead of time. Whether I like my room or not doesn't depend on how the furniture is arranged, it's how I arrange it in my mind. I already decided to love it.

Our attitude's growth never stops. Our attitudes are formed by our experiences and how we choose to react to them. Your surroundings and conditions as you grow up and the people you surround yourself with have a major impact on your positive and negative attitudes.

Ignore the negativity. The best makeup is your smile. There is no beauty like the one that comes from inside you.

The future not only looks bright when the attitude is right, but also the present is much more enjoyable. The positive person understands that the journey is as enjoyable as the destination.

The individual whose attitude causes him to approach life from an entirely positive perspective is not always understood. He is what some would call a "no limit" person. In other words, he doesn't accept the normal limitations of life like most people. Wrong attitudes in our lives will block the blessings of God and cause us to live below God's potential for our lives.

Everyone likes to put categories on when people learn things. From my readings, I believe the following categories best show you how we learn things.

BIRTH/AGE	ENVIRONMENT
1 – 6	Word, expression, family, parents
6 – 10	Self-image, exposure to new experiences
11 – 21	Association with peers, physical appearance
21 - 61	Marriage, family, job, success, adjustments, assessment of life

All these factors play an important part in our lives and can't really be "boxed" into age zones, but it is easier to understand when you look at it this way.

Attitude Adjustments:

When you get up in the morning and it does not start right – you know you're going to have a bad day. First you hit your toe on the corner of the wall, then you step on your cat's tail as you go into the kitchen, then after you get out of the shower and are curling your hair, you burn your forehead with the curling iron -- you might say it is going to be a terrible, horrible, no good, very bad day. On the way to work you almost hit a car that stopped too soon. As you get to work and are getting on the elevator the door closes on your foot causing you to drop your purse with everything falling out on the floor. You say I know I am having a terrible, horrible, no good, very bad day, and no one answers you.

> I learned from my mother that hard work will always pay off.

Here are some rules to remember when you are having one of those terrible, horrible, no good, very bad days and your attitude starts to plummet. Maintain the right attitude, "when the going gets tough the tough get going." Also, remember what really matters is what happens in us, not to us! Remember you can change your attitude by thinking positive and saying positive things. But the biggest way to change your attitude is by reading books and always being positive.

People see me as a very positive person today, but they would not have recognized me when I was growing up as a positive person. Before I understood what, a Christian was, my attitude was shaped by the world around me. My thinking was conformed to the world's values not God's values. I was reared in a broken home with four brothers and my mother. She worked two or three jobs to keep food on the table. Did we always live under the best circumstances? Not all the time, but we did pull through all the situations. I learned from my mother that hard work and a good attitude will always pay off. I started working in a grocery store with my mother at 10 years old. Yes, that was before labor laws. I bagged groceries and took them to the customers' cars for a dime or quarter.

I've heard my whole life that "things aren't always what they seem." Our attitude determines our approach to life. I know you have heard this phrase "Is the glass half full or half empty?" It all depends on your attitude and your outlook on life.

It is a shame, but most people around you in most cases don't care about your attitude and don't want to help improve your attitude. They cannot control your attitude -- only you can.

It would be impossible to estimate the number of jobs which have been lost, the number of promotions missed, the number of sales not made, and the number of marriages ruined by poor attitudes. Think about it - you probably know someone in one or all these areas.

Challenge: For one week treat every person you meet without a single exception as the most important person on Earth, greeting them with a smile and saying good morning/afternoon. You will find that they will begin treating you the same way. **Often our   attitude is the only difference between success and failure.**

Making the Best of Life!

John Wooden, the great UCLA basketball coach who has won more NCAA basketball championships than any collegiate coach in history, once made a profound statement about life in general. He said

"Things turn out best for the people who make the best of the way things turn out!" I think he was talking about the most powerful determiner of success: attitude. Attitude is a choice, not an emotion, not a talent that some possess, and others do not, not a complicated skill to be learned, but a choice. It can be a difficult choice, especially in the face of adversity or tragedy, yet there are those among us who are still able to make the right choice.

Think of attitude as a discipline, the same as staying fit or keeping up to date in a profession. You must work at it daily in order to make it work for you. I think the best description of attitude is "doing what builds our character and our life to the highest degree." The natural result of attitude is action. A great attitude produces an abundance of positive action. A poor attitude creates no action or destructive behavior. Procrastination is the result of a poor attitude. The way we treat people is a result of our attitude. The interesting thing is this: it all starts and forms our daily thoughts.

Thinking is like getting in shape. The more positive and productive thoughts we have the more success we realize. Earnest Henley's great poem "Invictus" is the ultimate reflection of the power of thought and attitude. The last four lines of the poem say it all.

> "It matters not how straight the gate,
> How charged with punishments the scroll,
> I am the master of my fate,
> I am the captain of my soul!"

"Invictus" is an autobiographical poem. Henley had an incredibly turbulent life. He was one of six children raised in poverty. He was afflicted with tubercular arthritis at age 12. His left leg was amputated when he was 16. He spent months in hospitals struggling with illness and he lost his only child to cerebral meningitis. Yet, he was one of England's most celebrated poets and playwrights. The author was writing from personal experience and his life is a tribute to maintaining a great attitude in the face of constant adversity.

Today is a wonderful opportunity. It affords you the chance in a single moment of time to alter the course of your history, to change the direction of your life, to make a difference. The special moment comes when you make the *choice*, when you choose to be among the conquerors of life, not the vanquished, when you refuse to let the occurrences of each day determine your outlook like the ebb and flow of the tides. From your first thought when you awake at sunrise until the last thought at midnight, choose to be a positive participant in the game of life and you will be one of life's All Stars.

Charles Swindell said: "The longer I live, the more I realize the impact of attitude on life. Attitude to me is more important than facts. It is more important than the past, than education, than money, than our circumstances, than failures, than success, than what other people think or say or do. It is more important than appearance, giftedness or skill. It will make or break a company, a church, or a home. The remarkable thing is we have a choice   everyday regarding the attitude we will embrace for that day. We cannot change our past; we cannot change the fact that people will act in a certain way. We cannot change the inevitable. The only thing we can do is play on the one string we have and that is our attitude. I am convinced that life is 10% what happens to me and 90% how I react to it.

Joy does not happen to us; we have to choose joy and keep choosing joy every day."

Feelings are normal. They change on a dime, they come, and They go. We need to understand this and learn how to live above them, not by them. That is "why" having a good attitude will help you overcome those feelings faster.

Listen, you're not always going to feel like doing the right thing. We're not always going to feel like being kind to a co-worker who, frankly, is a big jerk! We're not always going to feel like loving someone, who is selfish and non-caring. We're not always going to feel like zipping it, when we really want to say a few choice words to someone and really tell them how you feel. But remember to keep your attitude in check and you will come out the winner.

"Make it a practice to judge persons and things in the most favorable sight at all times, in all circumstances."
St. Vincent de Paul

Let me end this chapter with the Beatitudes from Matthew 5.

Blessed are the poor in spirit, for theirs is the kingdom of heaven.
Blessed are the meek, for they will inherit the land.
Blessed are they that mourn, for they will be comforted.
Blessed are they who hunger and thirst for
Righteousness for they will be satisfied.
Blessed are the merciful, for they will be shown mercy.
Blessed are the clean of heart, for they will see God.
Blessed are the peacemakers, for they will be called
children of God.
Blessed are they who are persecuted for the sake of righteousness,
for theirs is the kingdom of heaven.
Blessed are you when men reproach you, and persecute you, and
Speaking falsely, say all manner of evil against you for my sake.

Now take 5 minutes and read Proverbs 2.

Don't read another chapter until you write one thing you have learned from your readings today that will help you become a better person.

_____

_____

_____

_____

_____

_____

_____

_____

_____

_____

_____

_Proverbs 2:6 - For the Lord gives wisdom, from his mouth
come knowledge and understanding._

DAY 3 - WISDOM/KNOWLEDGE

James 3:17 - The wisdom that is from above is first pure, then peaceable, gentle and easy to be in treated, full of mercy and good fruits, without partiality and without hypocrisy.

Mark Twain said, *"There are two important days; the day you were born, and the day you figure out 'why' you were born."*

"Knowing yourself is the beginning of all wisdom." Aristotle

Song: *All You Ever Wanted* from Casting Crowns. This song captures the meaning of Wisdom/Knowledge.

Can you learn Wisdom? The answer is yes, wisdom can be taught to you, especially through the book of Proverbs in the Bible or through the book of hard knocks (life lessons).

Ultimately wisdom, or sound guidance aims at the formation of your character. Your character is formed by the wisdom you learn and value?

If you were not dissatisfied with what you have and what you are, you would never reach out for something more. So too, as one goes through the periods of darkness in our lives, all we can do is to put up with our blindness and wait for the light to come in.

One of the reasons for our sometime periods of darkness is that we expect too much. We are dependent people who wish we could depend on no one but ourselves. We had to face the reality that the world expected us to know something and to do something worthwhile. With that knowledge we are to make something of yourself.

Then through increasing knowledge we begin to discover who we are and what we need to do to move on. The wise stores up knowledge. Such an awareness of our true "self" and the world in which we must live reveals imperfections and difficulties in our earthly living, and it leads us to the next step where we develop the fortitude to continue our journey of knowledge. As we develop through the various stages of life (childhood, adolescence, maturity, growing older, and until death) we continue to learn at each stage.

> The past is where we learn the hard lessons. The future is where we apply them.

Sometimes the most important life lessons are the ones we end up learning the hard way.

Which comes first, wisdom or age? Some will say age comes before wisdom and others will say wisdom will come before age. I believe as we get older, we get wiser. So, let me ask you as we get older do, we get wiser?

The past is where we learn the hard lessons in life. The future is where we apply what those lessons taught us.

You realize that you cannot protect your child from all the evil out there in the world. They are going to hear bad words. They are going to see bad things. They are going to experience pain and sorrow. They will be hurt, emotionally and physically. No matter how hard you try, you can't shelter them because these things are all part of life.

GPS – nowadays everyone has a cell phone so if you get lost it is easy to plug in the address and you get to your destination. But it is not so easy with your life. You can't plug your life into a GPS, but sometimes you wish you could.

It can be difficult to define wisdom, but people generally recognize it when they encounter it. Psychologists pretty much agree, it involves an integration of knowledge, experience, and deep   understanding that incorporates tolerance for the uncertainty of life as well as its ups and downs. Reminds me of a story I heard: This executive of a corporation was driving to work one morning and had a flat tire, it happened in front a mental hospital. He got his spare tire and jack out of his car trunk to change the tire. He took the flat tire off and as he was removing the tire from the car, when suddenly he knocked the lug nuts into the sewer drain next to the car. The executive noticed over the fence that this guy was raking the leaves outside and who had seen the whole thing. The executive called to the guy raking the leaves and said what am I do to? The guy who had been raking the leaves thought for a minute and told the executive if it was me, I would take one lug nut off the other three tires and put the three lug nuts on the tire that he was putting on the car. You can make it to your destination without any problem. The executive told the guy, you are pretty smart, you deserve a promotion to head grounds keeper. He said no I don't work here; I am patient here. I am crazy as hell, but I am not stupid. There is an awareness of how things play out over time, and it is a sense of balance.

Wise people generally share an optimism that life's problems can be solved and, you will experience a certain amount of calm in facing difficult decisions. Intelligence - if only someone could figure out exactly what it is – it may be necessary for wisdom, but it definitely isn't sufficient an ability to see the big picture. A sense of proportion and considerable introspection also contribute to its development. To be wise is to have the virtue of being able to see reality as it truly is-that is wisdom. Foolishness is the opposite of wisdom; foolishness is being blind to reality.

One thing I will tell you: Never Stop Learning. The person who stops learning once they leave school is letting down their spouse, children, and themselves. Many men never read a book after they graduate from school and very seldom do, they read a book once they go home from work. Once you stop learning you might as well throw in the towel. You must expand your knowledge and wisdom to other sources or topics. To make a difference in the world requires you to take action. But action without knowledge or wisdom is doomed to failure. Even small actions can make a difference.

Do you think finding wisdom gains you benefits? What do you think are the benefits? It is understanding and prosperity. Wisdom is worth more than gold or silver. It is gaining the understanding on how to solve problems or situations and being a blessing to others. You probably thought I was going to tell you that with wisdom you could have whatever you wanted and be rich and prosperous. No, I can't tell you that.

From your Heart comes what you Think and Do. It is the internal thoughts that control you, not the external elements. "Apply your heart to instruction and your ear to words of knowledge (Proverbs 23:12)". Turning your ear to wisdom, inclining your heart to understanding (Proverbs 2:12).

The question I asked in the beginning- Can you learn wisdom? The answer is yes, Wisdom can be taught to you, or you can learn it through your experience.

Now take 5 minutes and read Proverbs 3.

Don't read another chapter until you write one thing you have learned from your readings today that will help you become a better person.

_____

_____

_____

_____

_____

_____

_____

_____

_____

_____

_____

_____

_____

_____

_____

_____

_____

_____

_____

_____

_____

_____

_____

_____

_____

_____

_____

_____

_____

Proverbs 3:13 - Happy the man who finds wisdom,
the man who gains understanding.

DAY 4 - CHALLENGES

1 Corinthians 13:12 - At present we see indistinctly
as in a mirror, but then face to face.

"It is not what we get. But who we become and what we contribute
that give meaning to our lives" - Anthony Robbins

> Song: *Hurricane* – Amy Grant – you will appreciate
> this song if you haven't heard it already.

Give me more faith, wisdom, knowledge, and understanding. Get
over my own embarrassment and reach out to a stranger who was
simply a friend I had yet to meet.

I thank God for where I was born, and for the conditions and
experiences I was born into. For those conditions and challenges
have conditioned my life and shown me where I was and that I

could make something of myself. I will never forget where I came from, and I think that is very important in life.

You never know where success might take you. Growing up I was always outside playing baseball, football, or basketball. I did not study much if at all. High school was tough for me and I was lucky to graduate. I went into the Air Force about six months after I graduated from high school. The Air Force provided a much-needed structure for my life. I started going to college by taking classes at night. In 1976 I had been in the Air Force for about five years and had just re-enlisted for another four years, but something hit me one day, if those people can be a Doctor, I can make something of myself and I applied for an educational discharge to go to college full time through the Air Force Reserve Officers Training Corp.(AFROTC) program at the University of Nebraska at Omaha and was accepted. It was a two-year program and I had about a little over a year's worth of college credits, so that meant that I had to complete three years of college in two years. So, I put together a plan which included day and night classes. During one semester I took seven classes. To make a long story short, I graduated from college in two years and was also recognized as a distinguished graduate in the AFROTC program. My senior year in college I was the Commander of the Arnold Air Society (AFROTC) and Speaker for the Student Government organization at University of Nebraska at Omaha.

This was the first time I was truly aware of God's hand on my life, but it was certainly not the last. I did not have an easy road to travel, but every time I reached a point where trouble was so deep that I thought I could go no farther, someone came along to help me through the deepest drifts. I didn't always know who these people were, but I always knew who sent them.

We all have struggles. If you have never had a struggle in life, then I would say you are lying to yourself or you have not been born yet.

I know you have heard the saying we all have our difficulties and our cross to bear, but you need to allow the light of God to shine through and guide you through your difficulties and put you back on the right path.

What's on your mind?

Well, when you think about where you are and where you wanted to be at this point in your life … are you there? What's keeping you from there? And does it really matter? Yes, it does, and you need to reset your goals and dreams to achieve them.

Obstacles and problems were never seen as opportunities for growth, but as challenges. I became a Christian while practicing the Baptist faith, but my life did not really change until I changed my practicing religion to the Catholic faith. You say "why" that made a difference. Sometimes I wonder if I can really tell anyone about how much impact the Catholic religion has had on me. First, I realize that God does forgive us for our sins and all we have to do is confess them during confession and once we believe that these sins have been forgiven, then our sins are washed away. I could go on and on about the change the Catholic faith has made in me, but the key in my opinion is my walk-in faith through the word of the Lord.

> There's not a person alive who has not experienced rejection of some kind.

Every challenge has an opportunity. How do you look at the challenge? Do you embrace it or run away from it?

> *"There's not a person alive who's not experienced the sting of rejection. There's always somebody – in the workplace, in your personal life – who passed on you because they didn't know that you'd be that good. Other people's choices and actions are entirely out of our control. But how we view ourselves is entirely up to us. Too many of us count ourselves out before we even get a chance. We can be our own worst enemies. Do the work. Be excellent. You'll find your place, and it may just be where you least expect it."*
>
> *Wake Up Happy,* by Michael Strahan

There's not a person alive who's not experienced challenges and some kind of rejection. We all have probably been rejected by the person of the opposite sex for a date or relationship. I know I was. How about being rejected or passed over for a job? Make the most of the rejection and learn from those mistakes or challenges.

When the time of adversity comes, what do you say about the situation? Anyone can be positive when things are going well. However, the way you respond when adversity comes will make or break you. What you say amid your challenges will have a direct impact on the outcome.

We all face challenges in our lives, but currently children are bullied more than ever. Famous golfer Tiger Woods was informed that a young man was being bullied because he stuttered. Dillon was a huge fan of Tiger Woods although he had never seen him play golf in person. Because he was being bullied so much, he wanted to commit suicide.

Tiger Woods wrote a letter to a young boy named Dillon on May 12, 2015:

> "Someone told me that you like watching me play golf. I really appreciate that, and I also want to say how proud I am of you.
>
> I know what it's like to be different and to sometimes not fit in. I also stuttered as a child and I would talk to my dog and he would sit there and listen until he fell asleep. I also took a class for 2 years to help me and I finally learned to stop. I was younger than most kids I competed against in golf and often I was the only minority player in the field. But I didn't let that stop me and I think it even inspired me to work harder. I know you can do that too.
>
> You have a great family and big fans like me on your side. Be well and keep fighting. I'm certain you'll be great at anything you do."
> *Tiger Woods*

Now take 5 minutes and read Proverbs 4.

Don't read another chapter until you write one thing you have
learned from your readings today that will help you become a
better person.

_____

_____

_____

_____

_____

_____

_____

_____

_____

_____

_____

_____

_____

_____

_____

_____

_____

_____

_____

_____

Proverbs 4:12 - When you walk, your step will not be   im-
peded and should you run you will not stumble.

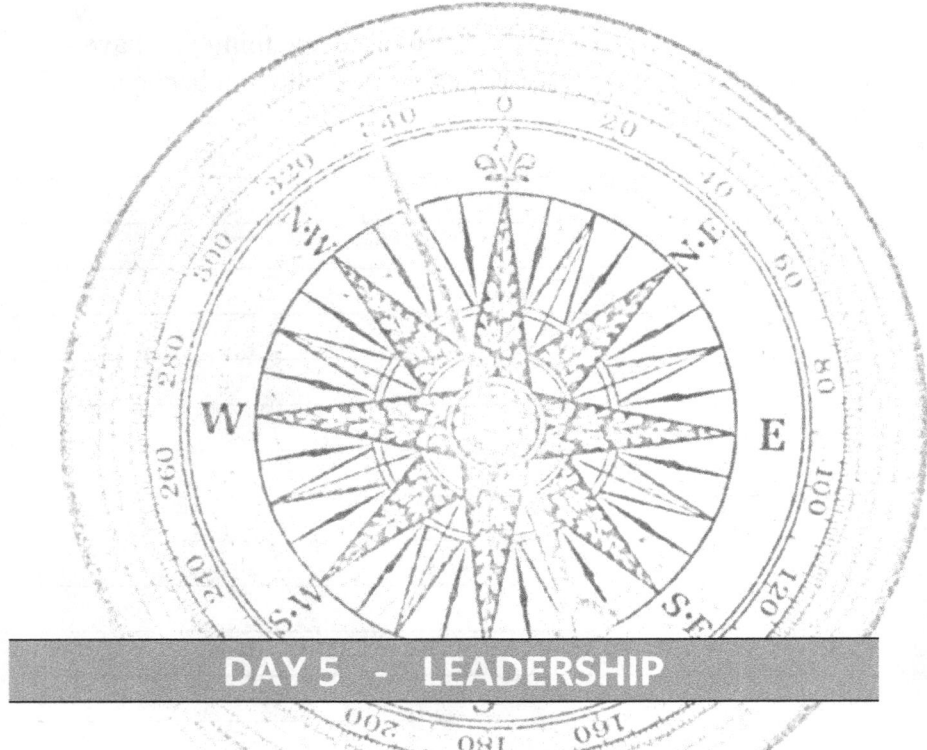

DAY 5 - LEADERSHIP

1 Timothy 4:12 – Set the believers an example in speech and conduct, in love, in faith in purity.

"You have enemies? Good that means you've stood for something, sometime in your life."- Winston Churchill

Essence of Leadership:
A true leader has the *confidence* to stand alone, the *courage* to make *tough decisions* and the compassion to *listen* to the needs of others. He does not set out to be a leader but becomes one by the quality of his actions and the *integrity* of his intent.

Situational Leadership:
Until you know what your strengths, struggles, passions, and purpose are, it's hard to have the confidence to actually have courage

because you might be worried somebody will see the real you. Courage is "leading into the pain of your fears to do what you know is right."

Today a Reader – Tomorrow a Leader – Read to Succeed!
The books you read and the people you hang out with will influence who you are.

Leaders are themselves often called "change agents," or those who are responsible for altering the course or direction in which they're going. Yet they also must cope with changes that do not occur by choice but rather are forced upon them by circumstances beyond their control.

What you are is what you will be and all you can do is to have the courage to accept that fact and make the best of what you have.

Leaders must trust and accept people they lead. You accept your leaders as they are, and they will provide guidance and discipline when needed to correct something. True leaders surround themselves with good people they can trust.

Teaching and counseling are two different things, but a good leader must be able to do both very well. I remember one time I was trying to counsel a co-worker of the opposite sex on some issues that they were going through and what I said was taken the wrong way. You must be very careful when talking to or counseling someone about personal issues. It taught me to never do that again. If you are being a mentor to someone and teaching them all you can, then stick to teaching and not counseling.

Throughout my career I have noticed one thing that good leaders do, they all take notes when talking to their employees to recollect accurately, to remind themselves and to review things periodically. Writing it down ultimately means remembering it. If you write it down, it also means that you are acting on it.

One thing I have noticed that there are not a lot of people who take notes when they go to church. You can always learn something in church from the music, the sermon (homily) or when you may be talking with someone at church. I do this all the time and when I review my notes, it's surprising what I learn.

Whenever you lead people, you must be ready to be adaptable and flexible. These types of leaders think beyond their boundaries. They are never satisfied with their current level of performance. I call these leaders forward thinkers.

I think there are two things that leaders do to excel – communicate and recognize. Outstanding leaders shine in communication. They make sure the people around them understand what they are trying to convey. Whether they are providing motivation, making requests, forming agreements or holding them accountable. It is a mistake to assume there is mutual understanding. The proof of clear communication lies in whether the other person fully comprehends what was intended.

Shaping employee performance is greatly helped by clearly expressing recognition and constructive feedback. You need to deliver recognition that works for most people. I believe that recognition or a pat on the back should be immediate or as soon as possible after the performance warrants recognition. Along with pay and work climate, being recognized is a powerful perk.

One who cannot be a good follower cannot be a good leader.

Leaders set the example – they must adjust their styles of leadership according to the situation that they are presented with.
- Autocratic – telling the employee what to do and how to do it.
- Delegating – works best when the employees are willing to do the job and know how to go about it.
- Participating – works best when employees have the ability to do the job but need a high amount of support.
- Selling – works best when employees are willing to do the job but don't know how to do it.

There are many almost-qualified people, but there is one success ingredient that is often missing when someone thinks he/she is a leader, and that is the ability to get things done and to get results. Ask yourself these questions if you think you are a leader.

Will you do the job?

Will you follow through?

Are you a self-starter?

Can you get results, or are you just a talker?

Reflections of Leadership:

I believe that every organization is a reflection of its leadership. In fact, the organization reflects the leader's personality, style, and most of all, the leader's vision. If the leader does not have a vision, the company or organization is a ship without a rudder. You might by accident sail the sea of adversity without incident, but most likely it will crash upon the rocks of change. Having a vision might be the single most important characteristic of great leaders! If that is true, then what is a "vision" and why is it so important?

Some would compare vision to a crystal ball that allows the great leader to see into the future. Vision is even more powerful. A leader with great vision actually shapes the future. He or she creates a future through the power of people and resources, something never imagined by common men. People are looking for something to believe in, something that can inspire them. Great leaders provide that inspiration! So, how do you provide a vision for your company or organization?

> An organization reflects the leader's personality, style, and vision.

Your first step is to stay informed of not only your own industry but economic and political trends in general. A leader who was aware of technology in the mid-eighties would have begun to move toward computers to run his or her business rather than staying with the typewriter. From 1983 until 1986, purchases of typewriters dropped by over 90%. How would you have liked to have been the president of a typewriter company during that time?

Second, invest in information journals and publications in your industry and in any related industries. Read weekly and share your information with your top leaders in your company or organization and your industry. It is amazing the ideas you will begin to generate from study and research.

Third, begin evaluating strategies for the future. A great leader looks at various possibilities, examines them in detail and chooses the best direction based on careful evaluation. One of the biggest fears of people is uncertainty. A great leader works hard at eliminating that uncertainty and showing a clear direction. Often, he or she creates a new future, not one imagined, despite ridicule and negative thinking. Fred Smith, the founder of Federal Express, had a vision that an overnight delivery service would be a way of the future. He was criticized for trying to create a service that was not needed. His vision created the future of a new industry!

The final reflection of the leader with a vision is courage. Courage to face the uncertain with certainty, to face the unimagined with imagination and to never waiver is possibly the greatest single quality that allows the vision to grow and prosper. The future of a company or organization is as strong and certain as the power of the vision!

Now take 5 minutes and read Proverbs 5.

Don't read another chapter until you write one thing you have learned from your readings today that will help you become a better person.

_____

_____

_____

_____

_____

_____

_____

_____

*Proverbs 5:17 - Let your fountain be yours alone
not one shared with struggles.*

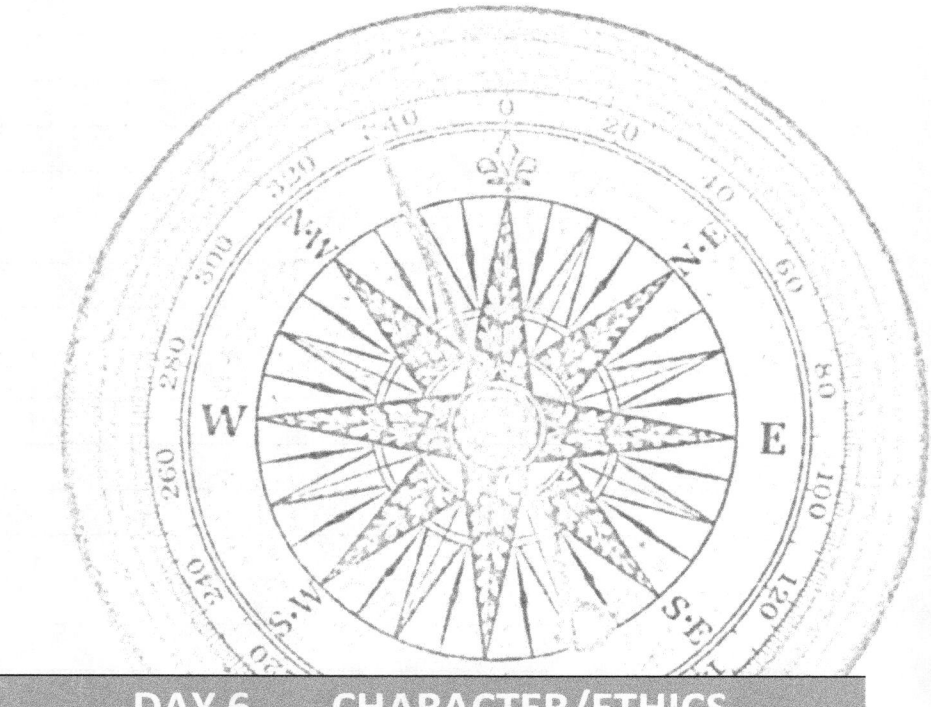

DAY 6 - CHARACTER/ETHICS

Exodus 20:16 - You shall not bear false witness against your neighbor.

Colossians 3:9-10 - Do not lie to one another, seeing that you have put off the old nature with its practices and have put on the new nature, which is being renamed in knowledge after the image of its creation

Character includes ethics, integrity and honesty in your life.

So, why do some people emerge as leaders while others don't? I believe that there are several key factors you can see:
- ✓ Character – who they are.
- ✓ Relationships – who they know.
- ✓ Intuition – what they feel.

✓ Knowledge – what they know.
✓ Experience – where they've been.
✓ Past Success – what they've done.
✓ Ability – what they can do.

Character - What makes people want to follow a leader?

Why do people reluctantly comply with one leader while passionately following another to the ends of the earth? What separates leadership theorists from successful leaders who lead effectively in the real world? The answer lies in the character qualities of the individual person.

The true measure of leadership is influence – nothing more, nothing less. True leadership cannot be awarded, appointed or assigned. It comes from influence and respect and it definitely cannot be mandated. It must be earned.

Temptation

We all experience temptation! We're tempted to keep our mouths shut and not tell the lady at the grocery store that she gave us a dollar too much in change. We're tempted sexually. We're tempted to ignore the outstretched hands of a homeless person begging for money. We're tempted to tell a little white lie for the sake of our pride or reputation. We're tempted to remain silent before the injustices committed against the poor and the powerless. We're tempted to lash out with angry, hurtful words against those closest to us. Temptation wears many hats and comes in different degrees, but it will always be around.

Sometimes we want to rationalize or justify the temptation.

- The lady at the grocery store needs to be more careful and learn how to count.
- The poor person needs to get a job like me, he would not have to beg.
- That does not concern me.

Rationalization and justifications are only excuses.

Honesty/Ethics (morals and values)

When you make a commitment, you build hope. When you keep it you build trust? Golfer Hunter Mahan was leading the Golf RBC Canadian Open at 13-under par in July 2013. Then he withdrew from the tournament at the start of the 3rd round because his wife went into labor with their first child. This was an example for all about character and responsibility. Family is more important than dollars.

Always following your moral principles.
Action reflects who we are.
Matching up your words and your needs.
Time is precious, but truth is more precious than time.
No such thing as a free lunch.

The person who is trustworthy in very small matters is also trustworthy in big ones and the person who is dishonest in very small matters is dishonest in big ones.

I have done many ethics training sessions for government agencies and organizations. The big question: What is Ethics?

E —   stands for EMPLOYER. You have a responsibility to your employer to follow the laws, rules, and regulations of your organization or company. Avoid activities that would compromise or give the impression of compromising the best interests of your employer.

T —   stands for TRUSTEE. You are trusted with money or company secrets and confidence, and you must protect them and not share them.

H —   stands for HONOR/INTEGRITY. Do not accept freebies; there may be something at the end. No matter if you work for the government or private firm, it is always wise not to play one person against another. If you do accept something from an individual or a firm, you may create the *appearance* that you prefer one person or firm over another.

I – stands for INDEPENDENT. Do not play favorites no matter if you are in government or in the private sector.

C – stands for CONFLICT OF INTEREST. Avoid any private or professional activity that would create a conflict between your personal interest and the interest of your employer.

S – stands for SOCIALIZE. Do not socialize with vendors (especially if you work for the government), no matter how innocent you may think it might be. The perception is 99% guilty until you can prove yourself innocent. I know the private sector socializes all the time, but it must always be on a professional level.

Six Ethics of Life
1. Before you Pray-Believe
2. Before you Speak-Listen
3. Before you Spend-Earn
4. Before you Write-Think
5. Before you Quit-Try
6. Before you Die-Live

Prudence – Moral Virtues
Prudence is a precondition for all other moral virtues. Prudence is defined as exercising good judgment or common sense. First, understand the problem facing us and then bravely choose the best way to deal with it. Any course of action must be based on a realistic evaluation of the possible goods to be sought and possible evils to be avoided as well as an honest recognition of our own strengths and weaknesses. If our choice is guided by prudence, we will not be too timid or too reckless. We need prudence in dealing with all the times

of our lives, our past, our present and our future. We must be prudent with respect to the past by "letting it go."
We can perhaps learn from our past mistakes, but we should not let them dominate our present.

"You can't bend the rules without putting a bend in character."
Scott Simon

As a new contracting officer in the Air Force I remember being told by a Captain in the Air Force contracting office, that you can always get things done without breaking the rules or policies. You must learn how to bend the rules and policies without breaking them. This has always been in the back of my mind. That is why I use the following phrase with the people that work for me: "What if and why not?" What if a policy or procedure needs to be revised or changed? And you ask the question Why or Why Not? What are the reasons it should or shouldn't be changed and legally you can change it and it will make things better, then do it?

> A simple lie, and you lose the trust and respect of everyone.

Trustworthiness is the most complicated of the ethical values and concerns with a variety of qualities like honesty, integrity, reliability, and loyalty.

When others trust us, they give us greater leeway because they feel we don't need monitoring to assure that we'll meet our obligations. They believe in us and hold us in higher esteem. That's satisfying. At the same time, we must constantly live up to the expectations of others and refrain from even small lies or self-serving behavior that can quickly destroy our relationships. A simple lie or any lie, and you lose the trust and respect of everyone. I can almost deal with anything but when someone lies to me, I have a very difficult time of even trusting them again. There is no more fundamental ethical value then honesty. We associate honesty with people of honor, and we admire and rely on those who are honest. But honesty is a broader concept than many may realize. It involves both communication and conduct. Honesty in communication is expressing truth as best we know it and not conveying it in a way likely to mislead or deceive.

Integrity – the word integrity comes from the same Latin root as "integer" or whole number. Like a whole number, a person of integrity is undivided and complete. That means that the ethical person acts according to his or her beliefs, not according to expediency. Such people are also consistent. There is no difference in the way they make decisions from situation to situation; their principles don't vary at work or at home, in public or alone.

> If we have integrity, then we have everything.

The greatest advantage of speaking the Truth is that you don't have to remember what you said. I can remember my Mom telling us when we were growing up, that if we have integrity, we have everything, and we can go far in life.

Loyalty is a responsibility to promote the interests of certain people, organizations, or affiliations.

People are not things, and everyone has a right to be treated with dignity. We certainly have no ethical duty to hold people in high esteem, but we should treat everyone with respect, regardless of who they are and what they have done. We have a responsibility to be the best we can in all situations, even when dealing with unpleasant people.

As I have watched and worked with many people who has made many promises, it has amazed me how many of those promises are empty words. Anyone can make promises based on what situation or desire they are trying to accomplish by the convincing words they say. It's our actions that prove our true character and actions always speak louder than words.

Integrity is Who You Are!

Now take 5 minutes and read Proverbs 6.

Don't read another chapter until you write one thing you have learned from your readings today that will help you become a better person.

_____

_____

_____

_____

_____

_____

_____

_____

_____

_____

_____

_____

_____

_____

_____

_____

_____

_____

_____

_____

_____

_____

_____

Proverbs 6:2- You have been snared by the utterance of your lips, caught by the words of your mouth.

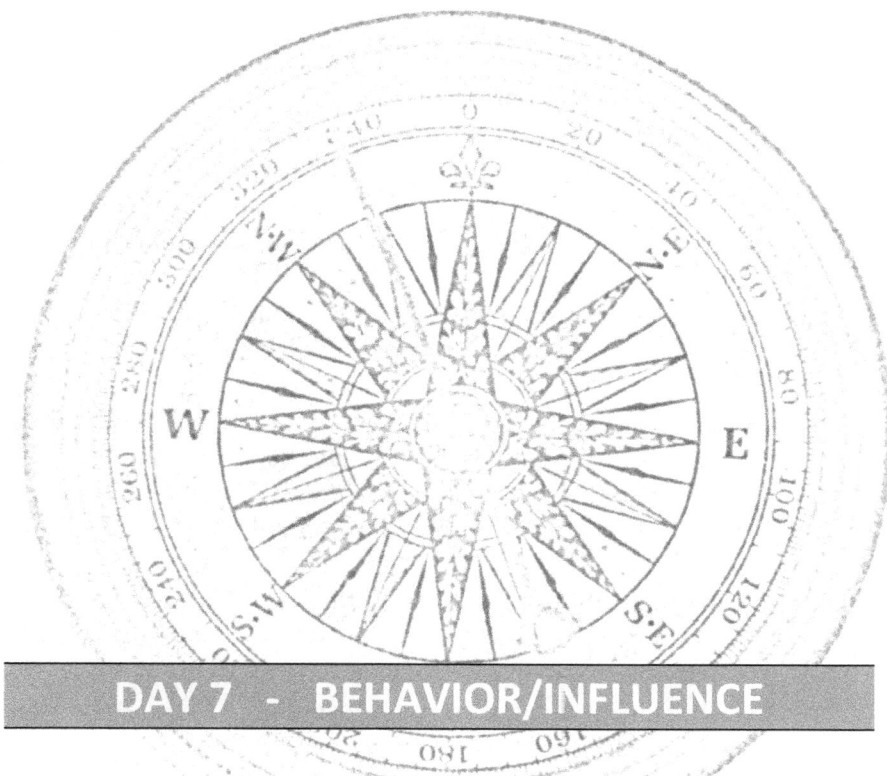

DAY 7 - BEHAVIOR/INFLUENCE

*Matthew 7:12 -In everything do to others, as you would
have them do to you, for this is the law and the prophet.*

*2 Corinthians 13:11 - Mend your ways, encourage one
another, agree with one another, live in peace.*

Songs: *Who Am I* – Casting Crowns or
You Are I Am – Mercy Me.
You may be able to identify with these songs.

Be with me, Lord, when I am in trouble and need.

The books you read and the people you hang out and associate
with will have a major influence **on** who you are.

Have you ever heard someone say they are backsliding? This
usually means they go back to doing old habits or ways of doing

things they did before, and usually what they were doing was not the best way of doing things or past behavior.

Influence: What you say and what you do affects people in many ways and sometimes you never know the impact on someone's life until years later. Father's have an incredible influence (positive or negative) on nearly every aspect of their daughter's life mostly. Father's need to very careful what they say and do that influence's their daughters.

When my son, Steven was growing up, I coached his basketball, baseball, and soccer teams. I was told I was a very tough and strict coach, but I loved the kids. Before each season started, I always had a meeting with the parents and players. I told the parents that if they did not want me to discipline their child and be strict, then this was not the team for them. I did not put up with foul language, someone talking back to me or anyone, or picking on another child. I guess my military background made me a strict no nonsense coach.

I remember one child -- let's call him Joe; he was about 10 years old and very hyper. He played on my son's soccer team and was at sometimes very hard to deal with at practice. Years later, after he graduated from high school and was going to college, he came up to me and thanked me for being his soccer coach. He thanked me for being a strict disciplinarian and for always being there for him.

> Learn from mistakes, but never regret making them.

Sometimes you learn the hard way. I remember growing up as a young child, on one occasion I thought I could be Superman, so I got a bed sheet and tied it around me as a cape like Superman and yes, I went on the roof of the house and with everyone around I said ok I am going to show you how Superman flies. I jumped off the roof and you guessed it; it did not work. I was around 10-years old at the time. This was silly for me to do something like this, but it turned out okay; I did not get hurt and I did not do that again!

You've got to take the good with the bad, smile with the sad, love what you've got, and remember what you had. Always forgive, but never forget. Learn from mistakes, but never regret.

Friends: Best friends must be able to give you honest, constructive criticism. If your best friend is your spouse/significant other, remember to always give them time to relax after getting home from work before providing any constructive criticism.

> *"True friends are people who come to find you*
> *in dark places and lead you back to the light."*
> Steven Aitchison

Surround yourself with only people who are going to lift you up higher and provide you with good positive feedback. Friends will be there for you when you are ill or feeling bad. Friends will chat together, laugh together, and do things together. They can disagree with you without getting mad or you are getting mad.

There will always be a reason why you meet people. Either you need them to change your life or you're the one that will change theirs!

We do not need sourpusses in our lives. We need people who are positive and who are always there for us. You need to be the light in somebody's life not the darkness in their lives.

Mark Twain famously said, "I can live for two months on a good compliment." Great for you Mark Twain, but I don't think many people can live off of 6 compliments per year!

A few years ago, my wife and I read "The 5 Love Languages" by Gary Chapman. Not too long into our read, it was obvious mine was "Words of Affirmation" – positive statements from others which affirm the good qualities we carry. But we forget how powerful a few words can be in the lives of others.

Here is my theory. It's not that we don't desire to share positive affirmations with our friends, family, or colleagues – it's that we either simply forget to do it, don't know what to say, or think it feels awkward.

I think the purpose of life is to be useful, helpful, responsible, honorable, and to be compassionate and giving. It is after all for you to matter: to count, to stand for something to, to have made some difference with your life and others.

With that being said, I took the liberty of making this easier for all of us – to remind you, to make it convenient to know what to say, and to make it so you need not feel awkward about what to say to someone.

Here are 10 Statements Everyone Needs to Hear
by Dale Partridge

Challenge: As you read this list, I want you to write the name of a person, or at least think of someone for each of the 10 statements below. Then email them or write them a note.

1. You've made me a better person – Who has helped you on your personal journeys of emotion, behavior, and maturity?

2. I've looked up to you – Who is someone you admire? Someone with a character and integrity you hope to find in yourself someday?

3. Thanks for being there for me – Who has been there for you through thick and thin? Sat with you as you've cried, listened to your struggles, and has never left your side.

4. I'm so proud of you – Who have you seen overcome a difficult situation? Or someone who has succeeded at something you appreciate?

5. I love spending time with you – Who do you have the most fun with? Someone who brings out the positive qualities in you, who makes you laugh, and leaves you feeling valued.

6. You're the only person I can talk to – Who is your special person? The one who truly knows you. Let them know how exclusive and meaningful their friendship is to you.

7. You're so good at that – Everyone is good at something. Think of a friend whose talents go unappreciated and let them know you think it's awesome.

8. I love you – We don't say this enough. Remember, people die all the time. Don't let someone you love go without knowing it.

9. You amaze me – I love this statement. There is nothing more honoring and humbling to amaze a fellow friend, family member, or colleague.

10. That's my favorite thing about you – Think of someone close to you. Someone who's personality adds value to you or the people around them.

Now take 5 minutes and read Proverbs 7.

Don't read another chapter until you write one thing you have learned from your readings today that will help you become a better person.

_____

_____

_____

_____

_____

_____

_____

_____

_____

_____

_____

_____

_____

_____

_____

_____

_____

_____

_____

_____

_____

_____

_____

_____

_____

_____

_____

_____

_____

_____

_____

_____

_____

_____

_____

_____

_____

_____

_____

_____

_____

_____

_____

_____

Proverbs 7:1- My son, keep my words, and treasure my commands.

DAY 8 - FAITH/BELIEVE

*Hebrews 11:1 - Faith is the substance of things hoped for,
the evidence of things not seen.*

*"Faith is to believe what you do not see, and the reward of Faith
is to see what we believe."* Saint Augustine

Faith is the knowledge – not the hope, but the knowledge – that our
story also comes out fine in the end. Sometimes it seems impossible
to hold that assurance. Personal tragedy brings doubt and despair.
Only by faith can we penetrate the cloud of human suffering to experience the knowledge of believing.

Pursue righteousness, devotion, faith, love, patience, and gen-
tleness. Faith is first of all a "thinking." It is not an ecstatic move-
ment of the emotions, a good feeling for no good reason. Faith is an
exercise of the mind, a judgment that "this is indeed so." Faith goes
beyond the evidence of reason, but it must still "be reasonable."

Faith as a mustard seed. When we know something to be true through faith but do not yet "understand" it, then because of our natural inquisitiveness we are motivated to try to understand it. Day after day belief opens the door to great virtue of knowledge that we only later come to understand.

Worry: If you can see it, you can achieve it. So, don't worry about tomorrow. Think about God. You have to ask God for what you need. And you have to believe not just say it with your mouth and your tongue. You must believe from the depth of your heart.

Live your life every day and everybody is not going to like you. Life is not always fair, but God is always faithful. You might be the only one left who believes in you, but that's all you need.

Sometimes you can't see something by looking directly at it, you have to look past it to see it.

Believe and Receive

Sharing faith with a spouse or child who is not interested: first you need to realize that God calls different people in different ways and at different times in our lives. It would be scary if at the age of 21 everyone had faith and believed, and they started to go to church regularly. God has his roadmap for each one of us and if we know that roadmap, we would take every detour not to use the roadmap.

> Life is not always fair, but God is always faithful.

Try to recognize the difference between each other's situation and your own. Accept the reality that everyone is not like you.

Go from looking at what you can see to believing what you can have. Don't undertake a plan unless it is distinctly important and nearly impossible. Don't bunt – aim for a home run, knock it out of the ballpark. The only limits are, as always, those of vision.

Faith in others – People's instincts are pretty good at knowing when others have faith in them. They can sense if your belief is genuine or phony. And truly having faith in someone can change their life.

As you work to become a person of influence, always remember that your goal is not to get people to think more highly of you. It is to get them to think more highly of themselves. Have faith in them and they will begin to do exactly that.

We all have regrets in life. None of us can escape them. But we can move forward. No matter what, God will take that burden off of you if you have a little faith.

A person who has faith without action is like a ship without a rudder. Faith gives us direction! We believers need to be people who put our faith into action.

Faith is believing in something when common sense tells you not to.

One day a 6-year-old boy was sitting in a classroom. The teacher was going to explain evolution/faith to the children. The teacher asked the little boy:

Teacher: Tommy do you see the tree outside?

Tommy: Yes.

Teacher: Tommy, do you see the grass outside?

Tommy: Yes.

Teacher: Tommy, go outside and look up and see if you can see the sky.

Tommy: Okay. (He returned a few minutes later.) Yes, I saw the sky.

Teacher: Did you see God?

Tommy: No.

Teacher: That's my point. We can't see God because he isn't there. He just doesn't exist.

A little girl spoke up and wanted to ask the boy some questions. The teacher agreed and the little girl asked the boy:

Little Girl: Tommy, do you see the tree outside?

Tommy: Yes.

Little Girl: Tommy, do you see the grass outside?

Tommy: Yes.

Little Girl: Tommy, do you see the teacher?

Tommy: Yes.

Little Girl: Do you see her brain?

Tommy: No.

Little Girl: Then according to what we were taught today in school, she must not have one!   *Source unknown.*

For we walk by faith, not by sight. 2 Corinthians 5:7

Remember every day is a blessing, a new chance to expect a miracle. You have to have faith that whatever you believe will come true, but maybe not the way you think.

For example, if you don't get promoted for a job when you really know you should, don't be disappointed. God knows when you are ready. It isn't always the best person who gets promoted because people select the person for the promotion and there's so much, they don't know. So, when you fail or think that you have had a tremendous loss, remember our Savior was perfect and his reward was a cross. And remember, as you travel through life with all its strife and sin, that as long as you please Christ, you're the winner.

We all go through things and circumstances that we doubt. You should really learn the 23rd Psalm by heart because when you say it out loud, God hears you and he lets you know inside your heart that he is being strong for you when you can't be strong for yourself.

Psalm 23 - The Lord is my shepherd I shall not want. He maketh me to lie down in green pastures. He leadeth me beside the still waters. He restores my soul. He leadeth me in the paths of righteousness for his name's sake.   Although I walk through the valley of the shadow of death, I will fear no evil for thou art with me. Thy rod and thy staff they comfort me. Thou preparest a table before me in the presence of mine enemies. Thou annointest my head with oil, my cup runneth over. Surely goodness and mercy shall follow me all the days of my life and I will dwell in the house of the Lord forever.

Now take 5 minutes and read Proverbs 8.

Don't read another chapter until you write one thing you have learned from your readings today that will help you become a better person.

_____

_____

_____

_____

_____

_____

_____

_____

_____

_____

_____

_____

_____

_____

_____

_____

_____

_____

_____

_____

_____

_____

_____

_____

_____

_____

_____

_____
_____
_____
_____
_____
_____
_____
_____
_____
_____
_____
_____
_____
_____
_____
_____
_____
_____
_____
_____
_____
_____
_____

Proverbs 8:8 - Sincere are all the Words of my mouth,
no one of them is wily or crooked.

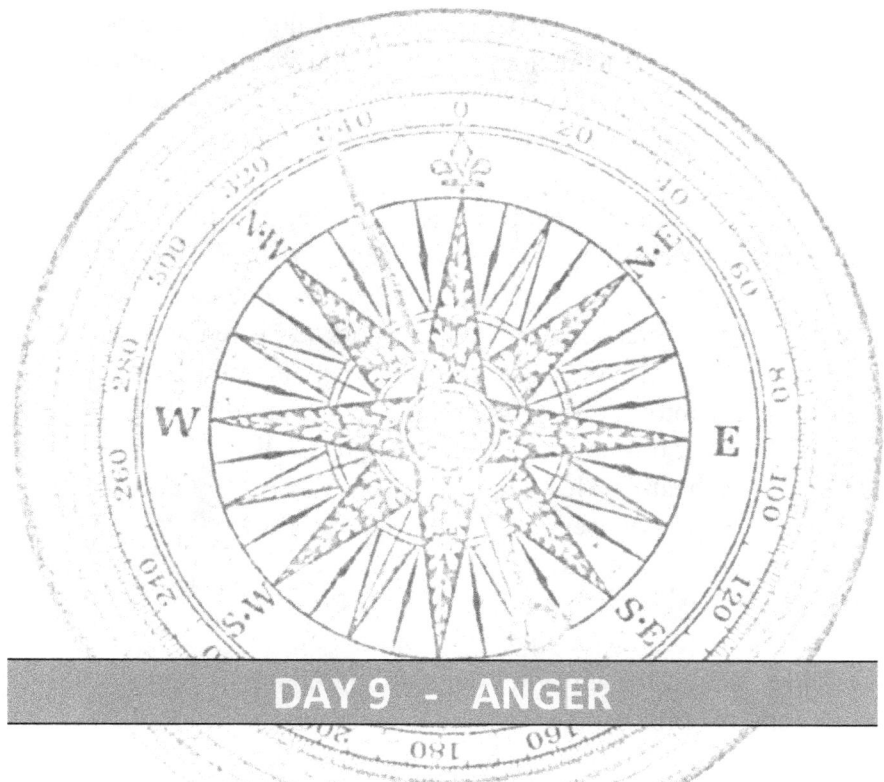

DAY 9 - ANGER

Ephesians 4:31 - All bitterness, fury, anger, shouting, and re-viling must be removed from you, along with all malice.
Ephesians 4:26-27- Be angry but do not sin; do not let the sun go down on your anger and give no opportunity to the devil.

Song: *Loving and Forgiving Are You, O Lord*
from Psalm 103.

Definition of Anger – Poorly understood, mental, violence, physical abuse.

Anger is a completely normal, usually healthy, human emotion. But when it gets out of control and turns destructive, it can lead to problems – problems at work, in your personal relationships, and in the overall quality of your life.

The emotion of anger is neither good nor bad. It's perfectly healthy and normal to feel angry when you've been mistreated or wronged. The feeling isn't the problem – it's what you do with it that makes a difference. Anger becomes a problem when it harms you or others.

If you have a hot temper, you may feel like it's out of your hands and there's little you can do to tame the beast. But you have more control over your anger than you think. You can learn to express your emotions without hurting others and when you do, you'll not only feel better, you'll also be more likely to get your needs met. Learning to control your anger and express it appropriately can help you build better relationships, achieve your goals and lead to a healthier life.

Anger can be caused by both external and internal events. You could be angry at a specific person (such as a co-worker/supervisor) or event (a traffic jam, a canceled flight etc.) or your anger could be caused by worrying or brooding about your personal problems.

> You have more control over your anger than you think

People use a variety of both conscious and unconscious processes to deal with their angry feelings. The three main approaches are expressing, suppressing, and calming. Expressing your angry feelings in an assertive – not aggressive manner is the healthiest way to express anger. To do this you have to learn how to make clear what your needs are and how to get them met without hurting others. Being assertive doesn't mean being pushy or demanding, it means being respectful of yourself and others.

Anger can be suppressed and then converted or redirected. This happens when you hold in your anger, stop thinking about it and focus on something positive. The aim is to inhibit or suppress your anger and convert it into more constructive behavior.

Finally, you can calm down inside. This means not just controlling your outward behavior, but also controlling your internal responses taking steps to lower your heart rate, calm yourself down, and let the feeling subside.

> For every minute that you're angry, you lose 60 seconds of happiness.

I frequently walk a three-mile loop around my neighborhood near my house and I have learned there are two ways to walk it. I can put my head down and get around it as quickly as possible or I can keep my head up, slow down a bit and take in the beauty. Also, don't be angry at the world, because when you say hi to your neighbors, they can notice your attitude very quickly. People can tell by your attitude if you are in a good mood or not or if you are angry at the world.

Similarly, we can walk through life in two ways. We can look down at the ground and wonder where we are going in life and we continue our meaningless trudge, or we can lift our eyes up and see the world and present a great attitude and be positive.

Frustration – how many times have I dealt with my children who were angry or upset and I said, "Now, is that really worth crying about?" I said it to them especially when they were young. I tried to teach them how to respond appropriately to frustration.

How can you turn disappointing news or outright bad news into a blessing? Read the excerpt from October 27, 2013 St. Peter Catholic Church bulletin below and find out how the Fowler family accomplished that.

> When an engaged couple calls off the wedding, it is usually a time of sadness and anger. But one family in Atlanta, Georgia found a way to turn a terrible situation into a beautiful one. Carol and Willie Fowler's daughter Tamara was set to get married at the Villa Christina catering hall, when the wedding was called off just 40 days before the event. Initially the Fowlers were upset to hear that the lavish gathering they had planned and paid for was not going to happen. Then they had a genius and generous idea: they invited 200 of the city's homeless to feast on the four-course meal that would have been part of Tamara's wedding reception.

The Fowler family called Elizabeth Omilami from the Hosea Feed the Hungry organization for help in getting the group together. At first Omilami thought she was being pranked! Carol Fowler said that even her daughter Tamara attended the event, adding, "She was also delighted to see and know that others had an opportunity to enjoy something, rather than just allow it to go to waste."

Children make up about 70 percent of Atlanta's homeless, so to make the dinner more fun for them, a clown was hired for their entertainment. The event was titled "The First Annual Fowler Family Celebration of Love," and the family says it plans on hosting another charity dinner next year. It's a great example of how you can turn any bad situation into a positive one.

Here is our challenge – to find creative ways to turn even our disappointments into joyful occasions. Be a blessing, not a burden!

For every minute you are angry, you lose 60 seconds of happiness!

Now take 5 minutes and read Proverbs 9.

Don't read another chapter until you write one thing you have learned from your readings today that will help you become a better person.

_____

_____

_____

_____

_____

_____

_____

_____

_Proverbs 9:9 - Instruct the wise, and they become still wiser;
teach the just, and they advance in learning._

DAY 10 - FEAR/AFRAID

Isaiah 35:4 - Say to those with fearful hearts, be strong, do not fear, your God will come, he will come with vengeance; with divine retribution, he will come to save you.

If you force yourself to go outside your comfort zone, something wonderful always happens. Always put your fears behind you and your dreams in front of you.

"Everything you've ever wanted is on the other side of fear."
George Addain

I did not have good grades in high school and in fact I failed two classes my freshman year in high school. Sports was all I cared about, and I did not study or know how to study. Going to college never entered my mind until I went into the Air Force and I started taking college classes at night. I found out that if I studied hard, I could pass college classes and in some classes I really did well because I enjoyed the classes and I was willing to study very hard.

When faced with situations, no matter what you face, God is always there to hear and answer your prayers.

Psalm 34:4 - I prayed to the Lord and he answered me. He freed me from all my fears.

Fear and Anxiety- What do you fear? Loss of your love one, loss of money, loss of your job, loss of health, loss of a good friend. The more you are anxious about your fear, the more you become overwhelmed by whatever is threatening to make you afraid.
No matter what's currently going on in your life, financial concerns, marriage problems, health concerns, concerns about your children, concerns about your job, concerns about your family. Remember this - the person who is not concern is the person that is not doing anything in their life.

Fear of the unknown – It seems if we do not know the consequences about something we are not as fearful. But if we start agonizing and make assumptions about something, we may be fearful of, it seems to overtake us. I don't have a lot of fear, but the one thing I am fearful of is snakes. I don't like them, and I sure don't like touching them at all, but I respect them.

Stop being afraid of what could go wrong and start being positive about what could go right. Nothing you have been through has been wasted – it has made you stronger and put you in your position of understanding.

Many people are so filled with fear they essentially go through life running from things that aren't after them. Fear of the future is a waste of the present. Fear not tomorrow. God is already there. Never be afraid to trust the unknown!

A famous old poem "The Prairie Pastor" says it best:

"Said the robin to the sparrow, I should really like to know
Why these anxious human beings rush about and worry so?
Said the sparrow to the robin, I think it must be
They have no Heavenly Father such as cares for you and me."

Don't be afraid to be you!

What does FEAR stand for?
F – False
E – Evidence
A – Appearing
R – Real

Yes, fear is real, and you must recognize it before you can deal with it. Most fear today is psychological. Worry, tension, embarrassment, panic all stem from mismanaged, negative imagination. Fear stops us from reaching our goals and dreams. To overcome fear, you must work on your confidence. No one is born with confidence. A lot of people fear water and swimming. We were on vacation and I watched a dad who was trying to build confidence in his 3-year-old daughter by swimming with her. She was wearing water wings (floats) to keep her on top of the water. At first, she was crying a lot

> Always put your fears behind you and your dreams in front of you

because she did not want to be in the water. About an hour later she was not crying, and it seemed like she was enjoying the time in the pool. Her dad did not give up on building up her confidence of being in the water. Action does cure fear. Don't let your fear keep you from taking small steps in your development.

What holds people back from expressing themselves and connecting with others? FEAR - fear of asking a dumb question, fear of answering the question wrong, fear that you would be laughed at or fear of embarrassment. I remember growing up, all the way from elementary school through high school and I did not ask many questions or answer many questions unless I was called upon and then I would not answer the question unless I was 100% sure of the answer.

The irony is that when you hold back from expressing your thoughts, you can still be judged. Those who judge you will do so according to who they perceive you to be as an individual, whether their opinions are accurate or not. What do people think of you? The truth is, they're waiting to see what you think of yourself?

One of the key ingredients in overcoming fear is self-confidence. How can you build confidence in yourself? Work on positive thoughts. Successful people know how to retain positive thoughts and forget all those negative thoughts of fear and move ahead. The best way I think you can develop positive thoughts is to read positive things before you go to bed every night.

"Never let the fear of striking out get in your way!" Babe Ruth

Babe Ruth was the Home Run King in baseball for many years and his saying not only applies to baseball but to everything we do.

"Never let the fear of striking out get in your way!" Babe Ruth

Action cures fear!

"Courage is the product of doing what one fears. Fortitude is the strength to keep going in the face of what one fears." Unknown

Dr. Michael J. O'Connor (chiropractor) – Dr. Mike as I call him – writes a monthly health and wellness newsletter. In an article he wrote he shared a book written by Martha Deck called "The Joy Diet." A chapter in her book was on risk. She writes, "Experience has taught me that the way to a joyful life is always fraught with fear, that to find it you must follow your heart's desires right through the inevitable terror that arise to hold you back. If you don't do this, your life will be shaped by fear rather than love and I guarantee the shape will be narrow and tiny compared with your best destiny."

Dr. Michael J. O'Connor wrote the following: "After all, there is a good chance that facing our fears and doing them anyway could lead to a smashingly disappointing move or a painful death!"

When considering a course of action that scares you, we should ask ourselves: Is this risk or action something that will lead me closer to my life's goals or desires? Do I feel a longing to accomplish this challenge or health issue?

If you can vividly imagine taking the big move and doing this scary thing, does it create an inner feeling of clarity and excitement despite the apprehensions? There should be little to no confusion or any sense of dread.

Do you feel only fear or is there an underlying sense of dread or toxicity? A good risk should feel like taking a dive off that 3-meter board into the deep, sparkling blue water. The same leap may feel like you're diving into a polluted scummy swamp or oil slick – yucky.

Ask yourself, "At the end of my life, will I regret taking this risk, or if I refuse to do it, will I always wonder what life would be like if I succeeded? Ask yourself what life will be like if you fail as well can you live with that?"

After reading what Dr. Mike wrote I can now tell you that, as an adult, I had a fear of chiropractors! I had heard so many stories about them, and I didn't want to risk seeing one and then feeling worse. Luckily, I met Dr. Michael O'Connor at a home show, and his wife and daughter were the ones I initially had contact with. I had been hurting for some time with my back and hip. Dr. Mike did a complete exam and x-rays were ordered on my spine and back. Looking at the x-rays even I could see why I was not feeling good. Dr. Mike started making the necessary adjustments to help my spine and alleviate the pain. He has done wonders for me. The fear I once had of chiropractors has disappeared and I can honestly say I am glad I took the risk.

Now take 5 minutes and read Proverbs 10.

Don't read another chapter until you write one thing you have learned from your readings today that will help you become a better person.

_____

_____

_____

_____

_____

_____

_____

_____

_____

_____

_____

_____

_____

_____

_____

_____

_____

_____

_____

_____

_____

_____

_____

_____

_____

_____

_____
_____
_____
_____
_____
_____
_____
_____
_____
_____
_____
_____
_____
_____
_____
_____
_____
_____
_____
_____
_____
_____
_____
_____

Proverbs 10:27 - The fear of the Lord prolongs life,
but the years of the wicked are brief.

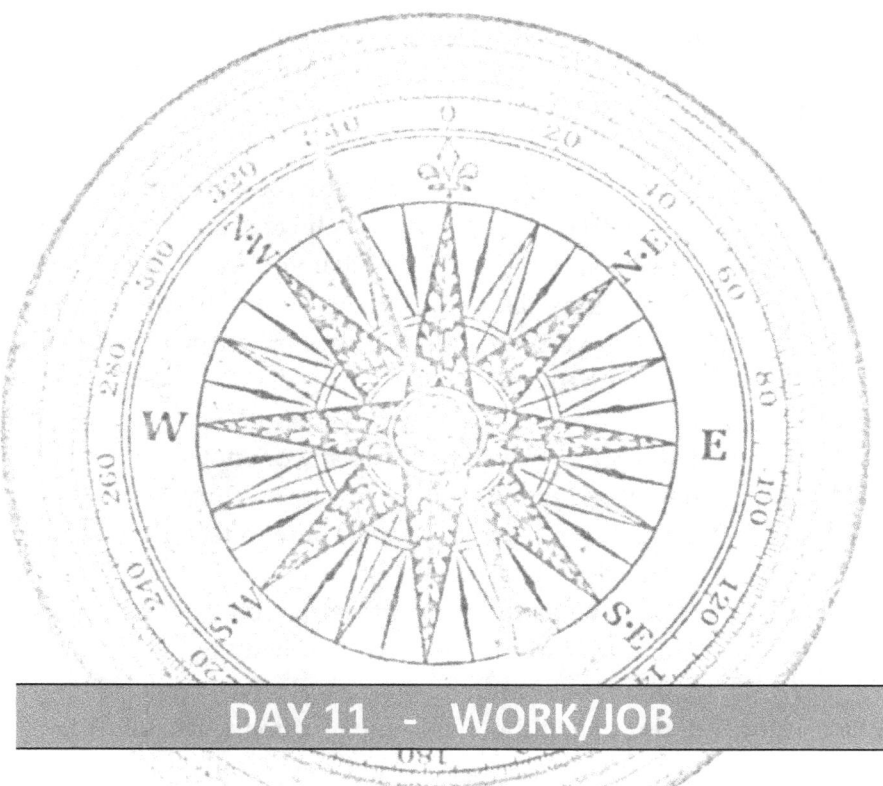

DAY 11 - WORK/JOB

Matthew 5:16 - Let our light so shine before men, that they may see your good works, and glorify your Father which is in heaven.

We live in a culture obsessed with material things. People work end-less hours to make the most money, have the biggest house, and buy the newest car. But when gaining earthly wealth becomes our focus, we invest too much in the temporary and not enough in the eternal.

Don't get caught up in chasing riches because the wealth of the world is fleeting. When we pass from the earth to spend eternity with the Lord, we won't take one cent we earned with us. This certainly doesn't mean we don't need to work hard in our jobs or whatever task is at hand, but material gain should not be our   priority.

Your mind needs exercise just like your body. That's why jog-ging every day helped me to relax my mind and think. I used to run every day at lunch time when I was in the military and my mind relaxed and I solved many problems, yes, I did relax when I ran. My staff at first was amazed at the solutions I came back with after jogging at lunchtime.

Your work is going to fill a large part of your life and the only way to be truly satisfied is to do what you believe is great work. And the only way to do great work is to love what you do. If you haven't found it yet, keep looking. Don't settle. As with all matters of the heart, you know when you find it. And, like any great relationship, it just gets better and better as the years roll on. So, keep looking until you find it. Don't settle for what you don't like.

You spend most of your waking hours at work not at home. That is why I enjoyed the Air Force so much because every 3 to 4 years they moved me to another base to tackle new challenges and make a difference.

> The only way to do great work is to love what you do.

We were better off when we were growing up and life was simple, and you had the innocence of childhood without the complexities and ambiguities of adulthood. As you go into the workforce and provide for yourself and your family some things have been lost and other things have been gained. There are ambiguities involved in the process of growth when you are developing yourself in the workforce. We are in the age of technological devices and social media which causes us to become aware of responsibilities.

Use what talents you possess… the woods would be silent if the only birds singing were those that sang the best.

Time is money, but you know you cannot get that time back, you only get to use that 1 hour once in any given day. No matter how badly you want that time back, it can't be begged, borrowed or stolen back and you can't earn it back. When it is gone, it's truly gone. Use your time wisely.

Excerpt from St. Peter Catholic Church bulletin 8/11/13

> Right about now if you are like me you may feel you have had it with email. Oh, I loved it at first and admittedly still recognize the many advantages, but there are days I just want to hit the delete button. I get emails from everyone. In fact, if not for spam, I am not sure what I would have to read. I like to know how they discovered that I need to lose a few pounds? Do emails have eyes? Who informed them that I need to go on a vacation? Hawaii sounds great but who is going to pay for it? I just can't keep up with my email. I have thrown up the flag. I apologize for those who are waiting for a reply; I just can't get to it. This thing called life gets in the way.

Some people seem to manage time surprisingly well; they squeeze more activity into an hour than the rest of us can get into half of a day. Are they better organizers, maybe or have they figured out how not to waste their time? I think these people have learned the secret to handle that issue, piece of paper, or phone call only once.

Nonetheless, we all run out of time. How do you spend your time? We all have different jobs – right – and we are all busy at our jobs. Now, take a piece of paper and list the things you do at your job – the daily things you have to do. Take about five (5) minutes to prepare your list. Looking at your job list is likely to discourage you in one way or another.

You might think you have a lot to do or you might think, what do I do all day? You need to stop doing things that really waste your time. How long is a minute? It's 60 seconds. Begin by timing a minute. In this part of the exercise, just sit and watch the second hand as it moves. Now that you've timed the minute, think about what your mind was doing during those sixty seconds. Did the time seem long or short? Did your mind wander to different things? What things? Get your paper and pencil ready for the second step of the exercise. During this next sixty seconds I want you to write down the thoughts that came to your mind during the first sixty seconds you spent watching the secondhand move. Now time yourself for sixty seconds and write down those thoughts. Did the second sixty seconds seem quicker or longer? Did you find that the two timed 60 seconds felt unequal in duration? It's quite likely that the first minute (60 seconds) seemed rather long. There was not enough going on to fill your mind.

Make sure you contribute more than you cost. Employees often mislead themselves assuming they should get to keep their jobs if they're responsible and do good work. Some of them even have the idea that sticking around for a long time makes them worth more to the organization. And we should not confuse longevity with loyalty. It's your contribution that counts, not the hours (or years) you put in. Quantity of work doesn't necessarily result in quality.

Prove your worth to the organization. Make a difference. Add enough value so everyone can see that something very important would be missing if you left.

Taking care of your career these days means managing perpetual motion – changes. Your organization will keep reshaping itself, shifting and flexing to fit our rapidly changing world. You need to know that resistance to change is almost always a dead-end street.

Change can be painful but take personal responsibility for adapting to change just like you would if you accepted a new job with a new employer.

In today's world, career success belongs to the committed, to those who work from the heart... who invest themselves passionately in their jobs and who reconnect quickly when change reshapes the workplace.

Instead of being a drag on change initiatives – one of the resisters who causes delay – develop a reputation as one who pushes the change process along. Make yourself more valuable. Lifelong learning is the only way to remain competitive in the job market.

Responsibility, power, and authority are being pushed down to the lowest levels. Holding yourself personally accountable for outcomes requires that you think broadly. Consider the big picture. Look beyond your own immediate behavior, beyond the specifics of your job description to see if you're really doing all you should to bring about the right result.

Organizations want employees who can cope with change without breaking stride. There are only two reactions to change: embrace it or try to escape it!

"It is easier for a camel to pass through the eye of the needle than for one who is rich to enter the kingdom of God." Matthew. 19:24

I dare you to be happy at work! Many people don't allow themselves the luxury of being enthusiastic, light-hearted, inspired, relaxed, or happy especially at work. This is a very unfortunate form of self-denial.

Happy workers are highly creative, charismatic, easy to be around and good team players. Unhappy people, on the other hand, are often held back by their own misery or stress, which distracts them from success. It's difficult for unhappy people to be solution-oriented because everything seems as someone else's fault. They are usually poor team players because they are often self-centered and preoccupied with their own issues. If they are successful, it's despite their unhappiness, not because of it.

> Unhappy people are often held back by their own misery.

What is the smartest career advice you've ever received? Have the best attitude of anyone in your department. I treat every day as a Friday. Why do I say that I treat every day as a Friday? Have you noticed that more people are happier on Fridays? They are smiling and laughing a lot more. I have always said that I would hire someone with a good attitude over someone who is always negative and who is a sourpuss. Always be willing to go the extra mile and be confident. Far and away the best prize that life offers is the chance to work hard at work worth doing.

Now take 5 minutes and read Proverbs 11.

Don't read another chapter until you write one thing you have learned from your readings today that will help you become a better person.

_____

_____

_____

_____

_____

_____

_____

_____

_____

_____

_____

_____

_____

_____

_____

_____

_____

_____

_____

_____

_____

_____

_____

*Proverbs 11:4 - Wealth is useless on the day of wrath,
but virtue saves from death.*

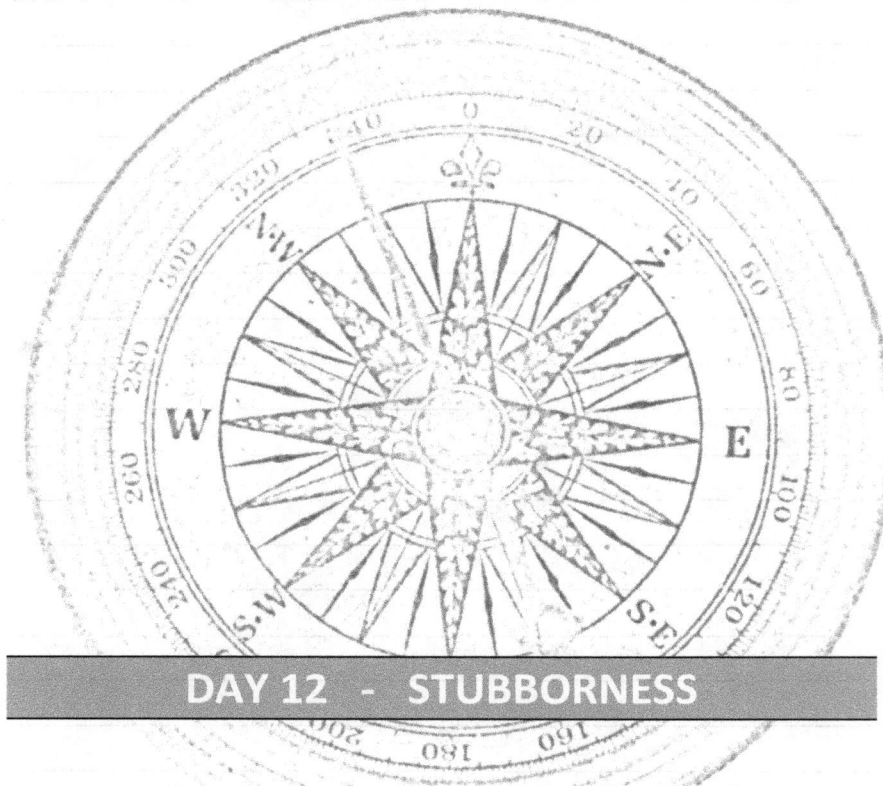

DAY 12 - STUBBORNESS

Isaiah 46:12 - Listen to me, you stubborn-hearted, you who are now far from my righteousness, I am bringing my righteousness near, it is not far away, and my salvation will not be delayed. I will grant salvation to Zion, my splendor to Israel.

"The only difference between falling in love and being in love is that your heart already knows how you feel, but your mind is stubborn to admit it."
Colleen Hoover

Stubborn defined: having or showing dogged determination not to change one's attitude or position on something especially in spite of good arguments or reasons to do so.

A donkey ride in the mountains seems like a fine thing to do until you have to deal with the donkey. Most of the time he cooperated, but when he didn't – he really didn't even when the excursion was almost over, and he'd been released from the equipment and his pen was in sight, the donkey stopped and like a solid stone wall would not move.

Why was the creature so stubborn? Didn't he know that the more he cooperated the sooner he would be back as the donkey farmer had put it "with his friends?" I wonder if I sometimes seem much like the donkey to my wife. She knows me and waits in love for me, but sometimes I know she wants to kick that stubbornness out of me. Why am I sometimes so stubborn? That is a hard question to answer sometimes, but most of the time it is the male ego.

"I am a bit difficult to be around sometimes. I can be stubborn on a lot of things and I am, but I can also adapt in a conflict situation and don't hold on to an ego. I end up seeing the larger good and adapt to it, provided it benefits me. I may come across as a cold person, but I am extremely sentimental." Emraan Hashni

Am I strong-willed and stubborn and dig in when people tell me I can't do something, and I think I can? Yes, I am. It goes back to my childhood when I had problems in school – especially elementary school. I was only interested in sports. Also, when I was in the 5th grade I had a major injury to my left leg (thigh). I was playing hide and seek one night, and the home base was the back of a truck with a big trailer hitch. I was rushing to tag home base and I caught the trailer hitch and ripped my left thigh wide open. The doctor did not think I would ever play football or baseball again. I proved him wrong, I played football and baseball in high school, started running in college and ran 5 marathons and many 5k's, 10k's and with my last half marathon I ran the best time ever at a 6-minute pace. That was my goal and I achieved it through some hard work and desire to do something others said I couldn't do.

<u>You may or may not heard this saying:</u>

Laws of Collective Stupidity: An adaption of this principal states that among people who are of the non-adult age, the degree of stupidity increases in direct proportion to the number of people gathered together. In other words, the more kids (teenagers) you have in one place, the more likely they are to do something really dumb.

I believe this especially applies to those of the male gender. But I have known a few of the female gender who do some really dumb things, too. When boys congregate, they manage to do things that most of them would never do if they were alone. Perhaps the concentration of testosterone increases their adrenaline which compels them to do something – anything that sounds bold and brave. But I think God made boys little dare devils for some reason!

Whether the reasons are biological, sociological, or pathological, boys feel compelled to find new and thrilling ways to impress their peers. When you question them about their antics "What were you thinking?" they respond with absolute honesty, "I dunno." The sad truth is that most of the time they don't know. I remember one time my brothers and I decided to create a wet, slippery slide inside our house in a hallway on the tile floor and it worked great until I hit my head just above the corner of my eye on the doorway. Boy, did I start bleeding. My mom was at work, so she had to be called to take me to the emergency room. She was not happy at first, but then she had to laugh at how creative we were to make the hallway a water slide.

Stubbornness is one of the seven basic character flaws or "dark" personality traits. We all have the potential for stubborn tendencies, but in people with a strong fear of change, stubbornness can become a dominant pattern.

Like all character flaws, stubbornness involves these components:
- Early negative experiences
- Misconceptions about the nature of self, life, or others
- A constant fear and sense of insecurity
- A maladaptive strategy to protect the self

- A persona to hide all of the above in adulthood

Early Negative Experiences: In the case of stubbornness, the early negative experiences typically consist of domestic instability or upheaval and the stress of having to suddenly put up with new situations. The situations causing such stress could be beyond the parent's control, such as having to uproot in a time of war. Alternatively, the stressful instability (as the child experiences it) could be of the parent's own choosing such as constantly moving homes to find a better job. Most often, perhaps it is just part of ordinary family life, i.e., the arrival of a new baby or when you are in the military and you move every 3 to 5 years.

   Whatever the circumstances, the core experience for the children in question is the shock of the new. Just when these children think they know where they are, living safely at home with their best friends and their favorite toys, without any warning they are whisked off to start afresh in a new, unfamiliar place. Change has been imposed on them against their will and it has caused unbearable stress. The cumulative effect is a desperate desire for stability and familiarity to stay put and have everything nailed into place and to fend off anything new or unfamiliar.

Misconceptions: From such experience of sudden instability and imposed change, the child comes to perceive life as being unstable and volatile:
- New situations are traumatic and must be avoided.
- People want to impose drastic changes on me against my will.
- A big enough change in my life could destroy me.

Fear: Based on the above misconceptions and early negative experiences, the child becomes gripped by a specific kind of fear. In this case of course, the fear is of new situations, of having new unfamiliar circumstances imposed upon oneself.

Strategy: Because of this constant fear, the individual will crave permanence, stability, and predictability. So the basic coping strategy is to resist change and any possibility of change.

Typically, this involves:
- Refusing to change or to accept new situations, when asked to do so
- Blocking the emergence of new/unfamiliar situations
- Perceiving and anticipating every possibility of change or novelty so that it can be blocked
- Denying that there is ever a need for change
- Resisting internal pressures or impulses to change oneself

Finally, emerging into adulthood, the individual does not want to go around being overly afraid of new situations. Hence, stubbornness puts on a mask which says to the world "It's not me – it's just this situation. Changing it would be wrong and unnecessary. Everything is fine the way it is actually."

Now take 5 minutes and read Proverbs 12.

Don't read another chapter until you write one thing you have learned from your readings today that will help you become a better person.

_____

_____

_____

_____

_____

_____

_____

_____

_____

_____

_____

_____

_____

Proverbs 12:1 - He who loves correction loves knowledge, but he who hates reproof is stupid.

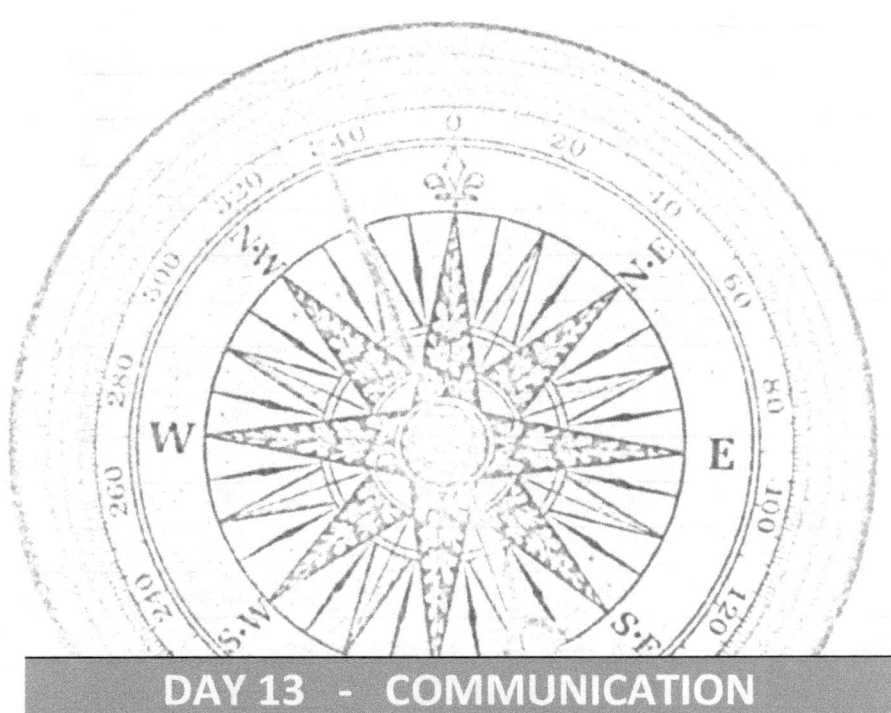

DAY 13 - COMMUNICATION

*Ephesians 4:29 - Do not let any unwholesome talk come out
of your mouth, but only what is helpful for building others
up according to their needs, that it may
benefit those who listen.*

People won't care what you say until they know you care! God
speaks to you in a way he knows you will listen to him.

The word communication has many meanings. Communication is both verbal and non-verbal. For some it means command of
the written word. For others it is the ability to speak thoughtfully
and clearly or being a good listener, or the awareness of good body
language.

Good communication opens doors; poor communication can
close them.

Communication is the single most important key to success in the workplace. If you cannot communicate with confidence and credibility, you may be passed over for promotions, have a difficult time relating to coworkers and colleagues and bear the brunt of misunderstandings and mistakes.

Have you ever marveled at how certain people always seem to put others at ease, are able to captivate listeners as soon as they speak and take command of a room as soon as they enter? If you secretly wished you had even *half* of their abilities, you're not alone!

Anyone can learn to communicate more effectively; all it takes is practice, self-awareness, and someone to lead the way! If you would like to hone your written skills, enhance your workplace relationships, speak more confidently in public and boost your reputation as a trusted, respected professional, don't miss any opportunity you get to learn and hear people talk about communication.

Good written communication skills are very important. Written communication by good leaders is clear, effective, and timely. Communication involves a number of things, including being able to speak and write well, to listen attentively, and to exhibit good body language. It is being able to respond to letters, phone calls, and emails in a timely manner. The best leaders, in my opinion, respond; usually within 48 hours, you should have some kind of communication with the person or persons associated with the communication that was sent to you.

Don't say a word:
Listening is the number one skill for effective communication.

The area we seem to be most deficient in these days is the art of listening. There is a specific reason why God gave us two ears and one mouth and why our ears are designed never to shut down or be closed, but our mouth is. Most of us are not good listeners. Most of us listen only long enough to shoot from the hip, to offer a little advice, give your opinion, narrate a few stories of our own experiences and go to another subject. When we are speaking, we are not learning.

What separates the great leaders from others is that they have truly learned the art of listening. The art of listening is not easy, but necessary to be a good leader. In fact, one of the most important classes you can enroll in is a class on listening. In my opinion great listeners also write things down when listening.

Of course, understanding (and even not understanding) the message pre-supposes that we first have heard it, and this in itself is a problem. With technology changes these days from texting, emails, twitter, chat boxes, etc. people do not take the time to listen and discuss issues. Everyone is in a big hurry! I can remember growing up my mother saying, "Did you hear what I said?" Back then I did not have all the distractions that everyone has in the 21st century. You must have an open mind if you are going to listen intently.

> **Listening is the number one skill for effective communication.**

Of course, it is impossible to have a completely open mind. There is an axiom from philosophy that states: *omnis recipitur secundum modum recipientis*, that is: "all that is received by a hearer is received according to the circumstances of the hearer." Each of us listens and understands messages a bit differently. Knowledge is not a process where all listeners are like a sponge waiting patiently to receive exactly the same imprint from a common experience. Our different perceptions of these internal and external worlds provide the raw materials. We may all hear the same words, but we understand them in our own way.

In this age of technology, some of the most used forms of communications are emails and text messages. You need to be very careful how you write things when using these methods of communication.

If you have trouble talking to people or starting a conversation, there is something you can use to start a conversation. Remember the word FORM:

F – Family
O – Occupation – What do you do – job?
R – Recreation – What do you do when you are not working?
M – Motivation – Who motivates you to do what you do?

Of course, although listening is essential to good leadership it is also necessary to communicate. Often when we think of communication, we think only of verbal communication. Let's talk about non-verbal communication. Body language is also an integral part of expression.

A smile is worth a thousand words. In addition to a smile we must also remember to laugh. It's a shame that children laugh so much and adults so little. Laughing is good for our health. Every time we laugh, happy hormones are released. Best thing for you- you need someone who makes you laugh at the drop of a hat.

Now take 5 minutes and read Proverbs 13.

Don't read another chapter until you write one thing you have learned from your readings today that will help you become a better person.

_____

_____

_____

_____

_____

_____

_____

_____

_____

_____

_____

_____

_____

_____

_____

_____

_____

_____

_____

_____

_____

_____

_____

_____

_____

_____

_____

_____

_____

_____

_____

_____

_____

_____

_____

_____

_____

_____

_____

Proverbs 13:3 - Those who guard their mouths preserve them-
selves; those who open wide their lips bring ruin.

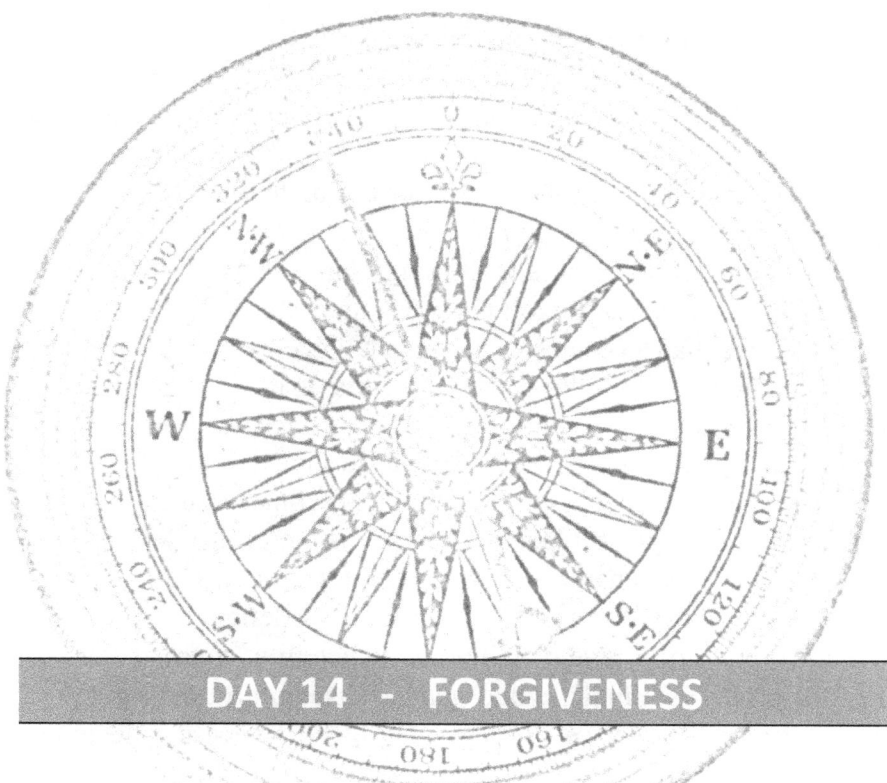

DAY 14 - FORGIVENESS

Luke 17: 3-4 - Take heed to yourselves; if your brother sins, rebuke him, and if he repents, forgive him; and if he sins against you seven times in the day and turns to you seven times and says, "I repent" you forgive him.

Forgiveness is about opening your heart and freeing your mind from the resentment and hatred you feel. We all know from experience how challenging it is to forgive, especially if we were hurt deeply.

What is your perspective on Sin? We don't have to be perfect right now to ask God for forgiveness. It's not a question of you or me first getting our act together and then being able to present ourselves to the Lord and saying, "How About Now?' Are you happy with me now? No God just wants us to come as we are.

The chapter of Psalm in the Bible has a lot meaning and wisdom. Here are some of my snippets from Psalm 103:

3. Who forgives all you iniquity.......
4. Who redeems your life from the Pit......
8. The Lord is merciful and gracious, slow to anger and abounding in mercy....
10. He does not deal with us according to our sins...

I also think forgiveness is the single most difficult thing to do in life. In fact, I would suggest that it is impossible to do sometimes. If you've ever had an enemy (person) that you don't want to forgive, but something keeps pulling you to forgive that person. You think really, you want me to forgive them for their actions. Yes, actually that is what you are supposed to do is to forgive and forget.

God does not keep a tally on how many times you ask for forgiveness on the same subject, or thing, he is merciful.

Forgiving our enemies may be the best indicator of a faithful follower of Christ. It may not be easy but is definitely necessary. When you fail to forgive, you hold on to hostility, anger and bitterness. It produces a malaise and general discomfort. We cannot be our best selves when we store up ill will. Forgiveness reflects the qualities of a good person, Christian or steward.

We might think it is okay to forgive someone who has only hurt you a little bit, but not someone who has really wronged you badly. But you have to forgive the little and big ones.

When someone hurts us, we should write it down in the sand where winds of forgiveness can erase it away. But, when someone does something good for us, we must engrave it in stone where no wind can ever erase it. Forgiveness frees us!

In refusing to forgive someone, you are closing your heart and love to that person. It does not matter how many times you have to forgive someone, give from your heart and don't keep score or track your forgiveness. Remember every time you remember a person who has wronged you, you have a choice to forgive them or stay upset with them, that is your choice.

Jesus said, "Let anyone among you who is without sin be the first to throw a stone at her." John 8:7

Of course, we all have sinned! Ask yourself: against whom am I holding a grudge? Decide today to forgive.

I like what Oprah Winfrey said about Forgiveness in a Sam's Club Article in May/June 2013

> *Forgive so you can truly live. Forgiveness is letting go so the past does not hold you prisoner and does not hold you hostage.*
>
> *Forgiveness doesn't mean you condone the behavior or in any way make a wrong into a right. It simply means that you give yourself permission to release from your past. It's accepting that it has happened to you – not accepting that it was okay – but that it has happened. It's not holding on, hoping, wishing that it could have been any other way.*
>
> *If you haven't been able to forgive, then you're holding on to something. The person who hurt you has moved on with their life, but you are stuck in the anger – you're stuck in the negativity. It takes a lot of energy to hold a grudge and be angry at somebody. The truth is if you're holding a grudge, that grudge is really holding you.*
>
> *We think un-forgiveness protects us, but in fact it really doesn't. It poisons us. It has everything to do with you and nothing to do with the other person. Un-forgiveness blocks you from taking the risk of love.*
>
> *Un-forgiveness unchecked becomes a cancer of the soul. What I know is that forgiveness is like medicine – medicine that can heal your pain. It can bring you peace. Forgiveness is something that you do for yourself. Forgiveness means that what someone did no longer is going to affect how you live in the present moment. When I got that, it took me to the next level of being a better person.*

Everybody needs to forgive somebody. Usually, the greatest obstacle is one person's unwillingness to take the first step! Decide today to be a forgiver.

It's the right decision to forgive for a lot of reasons including the basic point that it helps you most of all! Believe it or not, those who forgive:

- Have lower blood pressure because they are able to release the pressure,
- Mentally they are able to let their worries and concerns go,
- They leave their anger, anxiety and depression,
- They are more satisfied because they have released that hurt inside of them.

Everyone needs forgiveness. When negative circumstances cloud over your life and you're tempted to gossip, ask yourself, is this the right thing to do? Please remember that venting of non-productive words that rehash a problem only leads to bitterness. Focus on finding the solution, but if there is no solution break free from the problem and do not gossip. Remember, words are powerful and significant. They speak of motive and intention and they communicate much more than we often realize.

> Everybody needs to forgive somebody.

Have you ever lost your keys to your house or car? You struggle in your mind wondering *"now, where did I put those keys?"* You don't know and you can't remember. It drives you crazy because you can't figure it out. What are you going to do? You are lost and it bothers you. In our lives we make mistakes and sometimes awful mistakes and desperately want to come home and make things right, but you do not have the keys to get back in. You grow comfortable in your own little prison cell from your wounds, mistakes, or failures. You are looking for a key that unlocks a closed door and opens a new way you do not have yet. And you are also looking for that key that turns the catch or bolt to unlock the way to a new path. Until you realize that *you* carry the key and have always had it, you cannot open the lock. *That key is forgiveness!* Too often our past failures, mistakes and disappointments are too painful for us to admit and somehow, we are not able to let go of that weight and pain in order to move forward. Forgiveness is hard. Perhaps that is why it is underrated. You and I find forgiveness hard because we are *stubborn*. It is easier to do nothing and sit and feel sorry for yourself. Do you hold a grudge and have for some time? Until you fall flat on your face, you will not use your key of forgiveness to open the lock in your mind.

Forget about your past, if you repented and have been to confession, it's gone, it's in the past. God doesn't remember it, so Why should you? Have nothing to do with it.

Forgive and Forget!

Now take 5 minutes and read Proverbs 14.

Don't read another chapter until you write one thing you have learned from your readings today that will help you become a better person.

_____

_____

_____

_____

_____

_____

_____

_____

_____

_____

_____

_____

_____

_____

_____

Proverbs 14:10 - The heart knows its own bitterness,
and in its joy no one else shares.

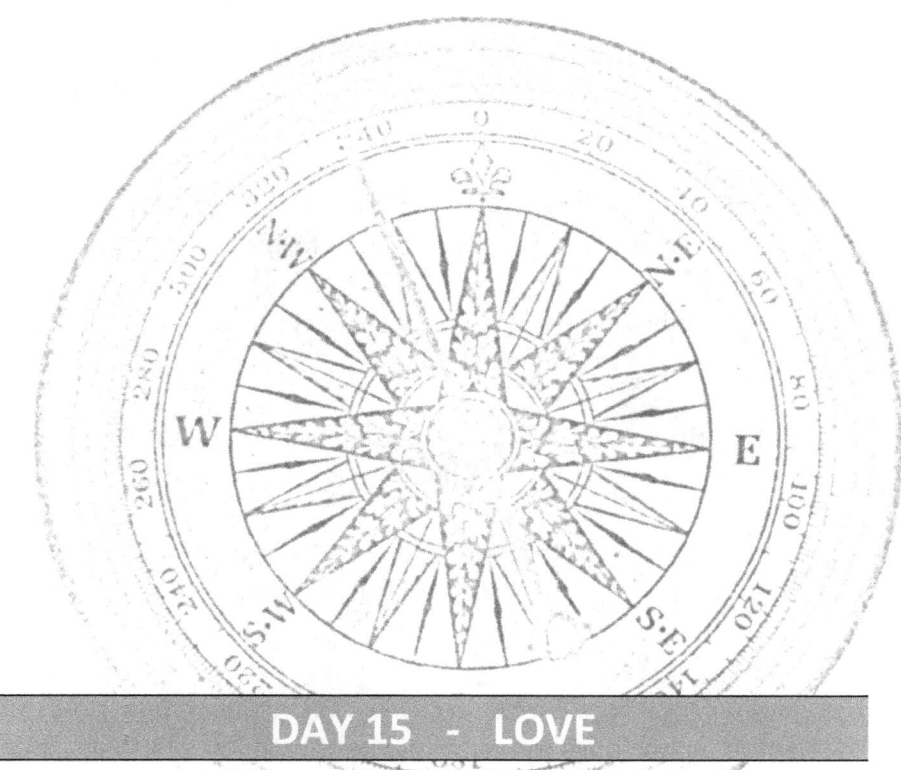

DAY 15 - LOVE

*John 15:12 - This is my commandment, that you love one an-
other as I have loved you.*

*Romans 12:9 - Let love be sincere; hate what is evil
hold on to what is good.*

Song: *Hold Me* by Jamie Grace is a great song that really makes
you think about the topic of this chapter.

Before you read this chapter, here is something you can do to
see where you stand; Read the passage from 1 Corinthians 13: 1-7,
substitute your "Name" for the word "Love".

1. If I speak in the tongues of men or of angels, but do not
have **love**, I am only a resounding gong or a clanging cym-
bal. 2. If I have the gift of prophecy and can fathom all
mysteries and all knowledge, and if I have faith that can

move mountains, but do not have **love,** I am nothing. 3. If I give all I possess to the poor and give over my body to hardship that I may boast, but do not have **love**, I gain nothing. 4. **Love** is patient, **love** is kind, It does not boast, it is not proud. 5. It does not dishonor others, it is not self-seeking, it is not easily angered, it keeps no record of wrongs. 6. **Love** does not delight in evil but rejoices with the truth. 7. It always protects, always trusts, always hopes, always perseveres.

When I substituted my name for the word Love I couldn't get past verse 4, without knowing that I had to work on a few things.

To love without selfishness and to forgive the injuries of the past, for only then will our hearts be truly open.

If anyone asks us to define love, we say that to love is to give. You are free to accept it or refuse it, but that is the only part of the transaction that belongs to you. You can't force love, but you can't stop it either. True love waits!

Love
Bears all things
Believes all things
Hopes all things
Endures all things.
1 Corinthians 13:7

Loving people love people. Those who have love inside can demonstrate love toward others. If love is not present in you, you can't give it to others. But, if you have trusted in Christ and have the love of God in your heart, you can love others even in difficult circumstances. Paul told the Corinthians that love could bear all things. Love caused people to believe even in the most challenging circumstances. Love produces hope and endures many hardships. As a loving person, you are able to love people no matter who they are or what they might have done to you.

You've heard it said, *"Love your neighbor and hate your enemy. But I tell you, love your enemies and pray for those who persecute you." Matthew 5:43-44*

Christian love is expressed in a multitude of ways: friendship, charitable acts, sharing our time, talents or treasure.

Self-Love: You have to love yourself first before you can love someone else. But you also have to like yourself. If you need to get your teeth fixed to like yourself, then go get your teeth fixed. If you need to get a nose job, then go get a nose job. If you need to get a face lift, then go get a face lift.

It is only through such loving compassion that we can hope to be like those "Blessed" described in the Beatitudes. If my attitude toward others is pure *indifference* my goal is not to harm them, but just not to be bothered by them. If I am indifferent to others, this does not mean that I have no interaction with them. Obviously, neither hatred nor indifference can bring me closer to union with others. The only force powerful enough to do this is the complex act of *love*, a decision to seek some good with the goal of becoming one with it.

If you feel good it may be part of the attractiveness of that person, but only you can make the choice to move towards that person. The pre-condition of knowledge and delight helps you feel comfortable with that person. You cannot choose somebody you do not know, and you would not want to be with someone who does not delight you. Without knowledge and delight in the other person you will never come to be with them and if you are not fully loving them you will not be drawn to become one with them.

The goal of love is unions. To love someone means to wish to be united with them, to make them oneness. When you fall in love with someone you want to rush to them and hug them with a powerful embrace, crushing their loneliness into the gap, the hunger, the thirst that their gracefulness has caused in us.

When you are overcome with love for another, it is like coming upon a pool of cool spring water on a hot day and wishing to jump in and be immersed in the delight. This loving union is clearly quite different from just knowing them. When you love someone, they are always on your mind. Your life changes when you love someone. When you love someone, your heart begins to beat fast every time you see them, meaning your love is in your heart not just in your head. To just know another will not make you love them, they must also delight you. You must enjoy being around them and find them delightful. Delight is what drives you to seek them and be with them rather than with another person.

Benevolent *agape* love is the highest form of love, a love whereby you seek nothing for yourself but only for your beloved.

Friendly Love: To live a somewhat happy life you need two things which are essential: good health and good friends. It is only through the love of friendship that we can become one with others. We may begin loving them because of the pleasure they give to us, but if our love is to be lasting and true, we must love them with the love of friendship.

Friendship can only exist when it is the highest form of love, a love of benevolence, a love which literally wishes others well. This does not mean that friends will always agree, but at least they must always care for each other, be there when you need them, desiring that only good things will happen to the one they love. A love of friendship must be altruistic, valuing the good that is my loved one rather that the good or the pleasure that they bring to me. Such love cannot be a jealous love. When I value them for what they are in themselves, I am not upset when they also love others.

It is our nature to need human friends, but to find them is a difficult task. When those we love are the last thing we think of at night and the first thing we think of in the morning, they are never far away. We can love (desire) many things without any return of love, but to be a friend to another demands that they also be friends to us. Friendship cannot exist with someone who does not know us or does not care about us.

On the practical level, to be a friend of another means that we must be willing to bear their burden and to allow them to bear ours.

A love offered to our friends in their good times is not tempted to subordinate them because of the good that they are. But, in this life the ideal state where friends never "need" each other does not last very long.

Bad things happen and it is then that friendship is tested. As we go through life, we are like a person trying to swim against a riptide (strong current) and not making any progress and sometimes we are called upon to take the lead. There comes a time in life when each of us needs a place to rest our weary heads and bodies and there is no better place than in the arms of one who truly loves us.

Friends may be delightfully sunny and breezy in good times, but if they go away at the first threat of a storm, they are not true friends at all. The problem with trying to develop a love of friendship with others is that we do not know them very well. If you don't know the real "them" and they do not know the real "you," our supposed friendship will be fragile.

That is the reason that maintaining a real friendship with another person will always be a difficult and demanding task. Our knowledge of them will always be imperfect. Even if we know what they are today, their desires and fears, their passions and their convictions tomorrow may be different.

Since we cannot know what is going on inside others, friendship must be based on trust. Our trust must be so strong that we dare to be frank with each other, free to say what we like and dislike about each other, free to share passions, fears, hopes, and dreams.

Since friendship will always be a relationship between *"cracked"* individuals we must expect those we love will never live up to our expectations perfectly. Sometimes they will do the wrong things, sometimes they will wrong us. In such situations, the sign of our friendly love will be our willingness to forgive them for the past and hope for a better future.

Joy of Love: For a while you are hidden from me and I tell my heart to be brave, but it does not pay attention. I am glad that I can't stop being happy when you are with me and can't stop crying when you are far away. Now when you are far away my only consolation is embracing my sadness.

Sometimes joy and sometimes heartache comes when we are deeply in love with another person. In such intimate love, though each is possessed by the other, neither is consumed. Indeed, a lover's individuality and freedom is enhanced by the expansion of spirit that the beloved causes. You cannot force your beloved to completely immerse themselves in you because you can never be more than a part of their lives. So too, you cannot give yourself totally to them because they can only be a part of your life. Even if you have a life-time romance, you can still only clutch a piece of each other's lives. This is part of the pain of being loved by and loving another person.

Sad to say, even the greatest love between two people is a fragile thing. Even a slight tug of selfishness can separate us. Hurt feelings, misunderstandings, foolish and misdirected passion, pride… These are the fingers that untie the knots of affection that bind us to each other. Even simple indifference causes our bonds to dry up and rot. To be tied to another by love needs constant care, a weaving and re-weaving of joined lives. Without attention and nourishing, the connection can break, and you can drift apart without even realizing it. The joy of having a true love is that they will love you despite your cracks. A true love is one before whom we can stand naked without fear of laughter or horror. The great joy in loving and being loved is that when we are embraced by one who really loves us, we know it is because they really do care for us. Such love brings a quiet calm into our lives. Though intimate, it need not have constant verbal communication. To rest in the arms of a beloved is a quiet thing, as close to becoming one with them as we can make it. Our hearts beat in unison and our spirits join together. We face the world now not as two but one.

> A true love will love you despite your cracks.

Pain of Love: It may seem strange to talk about the wonderful experience of love as a cause of pain, but so often it is. Even the most perfect love brings its own share of trials and tribulations. This is an imperfect world and no matter how devoted lovers want to be, they are hindered by the fact that they too are imperfect.

Love can be especially painful when it is not returned. That great "love of your life" may be quite pleasant about it, but it quickly becomes clear that they have no desire for the "intimate" union of hearts that you so desperately desire. It is even worse when the pain of love's absence comes from a love that once was but has now faded. Sometimes this happens even to the most passionate love affair. The deep affection that before bound the lovers together has now faded. The fact of the matter is that sometimes love does fade. Oh, it may still be a raging fire in our hearts, but it has obviously cooled in the heart of our beloved. The object of our affection suddenly becomes the cause of our dejection. Great love affairs are sometimes dissipated by changing places, changing times, and changing lives.

There can be great pain in such experiences if we honestly (and foolishly) believed that indeed "absence would make the heart grow fonder." Even when our love stays strong over the years there are still occasions when it can cause great pain. For instance, there are the times when we see that things are going badly for those we love, and we can do nothing about it.

When we truly love someone, their joy becomes our joy; their pain becomes our pain. They are truly part of us, and we share their pain. The cruel paradox of human love is that you can always make your loved one's weep. You cannot always make them smile. Love tears down all defenses. It leaves you naked and exposed to the least soothing causes and to the worst wounding blow. Love wounds may be unintentional, but this does not prevent them from being deep and piercing, with jagged edges. So tender are such wounds that it is sometimes impossible to make amends without inflicting new pain. Still, all things considered the pain that at times comes from having a passionate and deep love for another human is much less than the cheerless pains of those unhappy souls who have never experienced such love.

Love tears down all defenses.

Loving other human beings is a precious blessing in this life, but there are many obstacles that must be overcome before it can become this "right sort" of love. Because we are "cracked" we have the tendency to "mess up" even the best of our human loves by our extreme selfishness it is natural for us to "love" ourselves, but too much love for one's self stands in the way of any true love of others.

Inordinate attention to self is the root of a destructive pride that makes us believe that we are better than everyone else, that we stand on the pinnacle of the mountain while others live out their lives in the mediocrity of the valley below.

True Love Cannot Exist: When we desire another *as an object of pleasure*, desired only because they satisfy our physical or emotional needs.

When we desire another *as someone to dominate*, someone we can treat as a slave in order to prove to the skeptical world that we are indeed a superior creation.

When we desire another *as a trophy or possession* to be displayed to an appreciative crowd so that they might marvel at such an extraordinary ornamental being possessed by an ordinary person.

When we desire another *so obsessively* that we become incapable of loving anyone beyond them. Loving our human loves, we have no time or energy to love a Divine Friend.

Another obstacle to true love is jealousy. When you are jealous of another, you see them receiving a good which you want exclusively for yourself. A lover may become jealous of other loving relationships that their beloved may have. A jealous spouse may become upset by any love not directed at them. They get angry when their partner is concerned about relatives, when they go out of town with friends, or when they take care of the children. Such jealousy is destructive of love because at its root is a lack of trust -- that quality which is so essential for a true love of friendship. If our love is infected by a suspicion that our beloved is not totally

> God provides for our needs at just the right moment.

committed to us, that they are "sharing of hearts" with others you begin to consider them the enemy.

I would like to share a quote from a birthday card that my wife, Michele gave me on my 62nd birthday.

> When love is right
> You see it
> In each other eyes,
> You feel it
> In each other's arms.
> You taste it
> In each other's kiss,
> When love is right
> You hold on to it
> With all your heart and soul

When children get to a certain age, they must be left to go their own way. All the talking in the world will not change them. They must be left (and sometimes fail) to take responsibility for their lives, hoping that a memory of their loving upbringing will eventually help them straighten out their lives.

God provides for our needs at just the right moment. You can't force love... but you can't stop it either.

Let me ask you a few questions;

1. When was the last time that someone made you feel loved?
2. Have you ever reached out to a stranger to make them feel loved?
3. Have you ever had someone, not family, tell you how much you touched their life without realizing it?

Now take 5 minutes and read Proverbs 15.

Don't read another chapter until you write one thing you have learned from your readings today that will help you become a   better person.

_____

_____

_____

_____

_____

_____

_____

_____

_____

_____

_____

_____

_____

_____

_____

_____

_____

_____

_____

_____

_____

_____

_____

Proverbs 15:9 - The way of the wicked is an abomination to the Lord, but he loves the man who pursues virtue.

*Mom, Anna Belle Kersey,
as a teenager, around 1945*

*Growing up in Bunnell, Florida; Cliff, Wayne, George, Me, & Jack
(Where did the horse go?)*

My brothers and me about 1957:
front — George, Wayne, & me;
back — Cliff & Jack.

My high school graduation picture —
1970

Front, left to right: Jack, George, & Wayne.

Back: Cliff & me. Taken around 1959

*Promoted to
Major in the
USAF in 1988*

*With my step-dad, Ed Whitten, and Mom
at my retirement party from the USAF*

2005 Board of Directors of the Florida Association Public Procurement Officials; Dave Nash, Cheri Alexander, me, Denise Schneider, & Marian Pace. I was President for 2005-06.

2015 outside the Hernando County Courthouse with the Hernando County Administrator, Len Sossamon (in the middle) and the Assistant County Administrators from left to right: George Zoettlein, Ron Pianta, me, & Brian Malmberg.

At my daughter, Crystal's wedding with her husband, Jon Baily McGuire, me, and my wife Michele.

At the 2015 Florida / Georgia football game with my daughter Crystal and son Steven.

Relaxing at Hilton Head, SC with my son, Steven,
and his fiancé, Sami and her daughter, Alyssa.

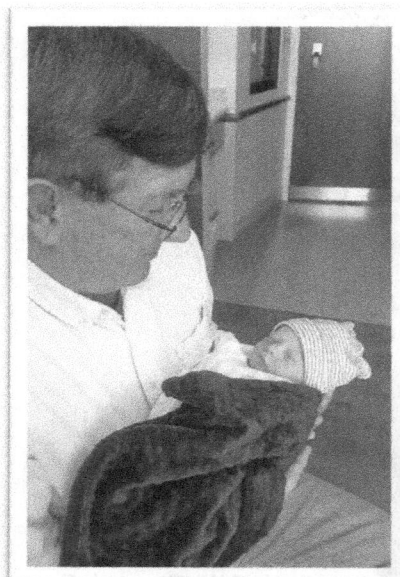

Grandpa Russ with his first grand-
son, Jon Baily McGuire III — 2/8/16

Michele's son, Dominic &
Grandchildren, Haily & Gunner.

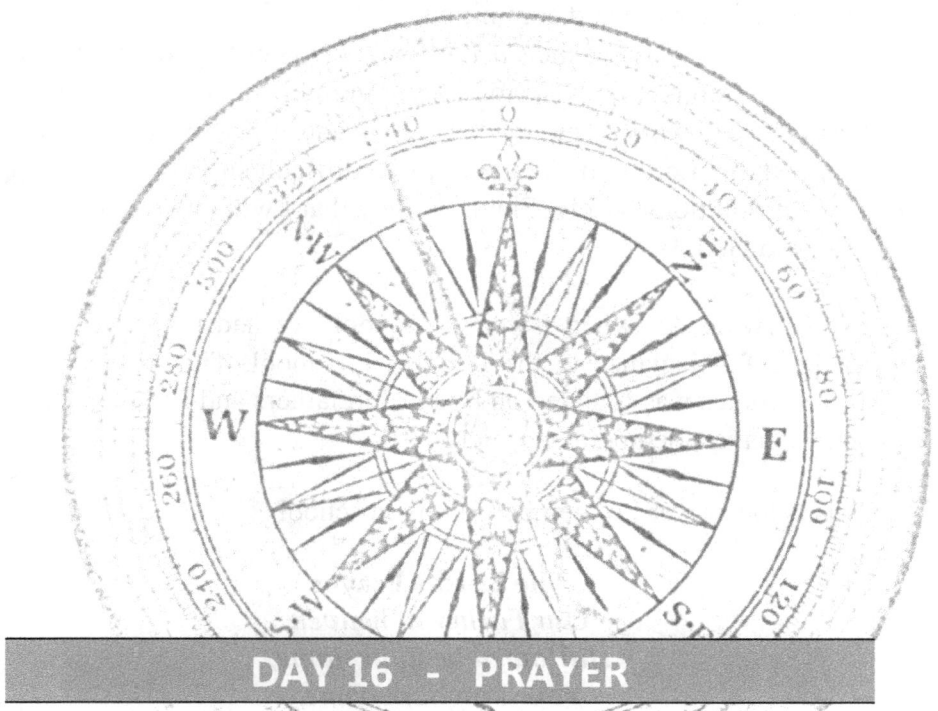

DAY 16 - PRAYER

Philippians 4:6-7 - Don't worry about anything, instead pray about everything. Tell God what you need, and thank him for all he has done, if you do this, you will experience God's peace, which is far more wonderful than the human mind can understand.

The strongest action that you can take in any situation is to go to your knees and ask God for help. It is better to pray badly, then not to pray at all, pray from the heart.

I like this quote I have seen it many times on church billboards:

"7 days without prayer makes 1 weak!"

Prayer is my secret to whatever success I have experienced in my life. I am always working at improving my prayer life. If you want a personal change in your life, learn to pray the four C's: careful, confident, calm and committed.

I ask God to make me *Careful* so that whatever I do, I will do it well and exercise care towards people in my behavior and attitude. I pray to be *Confident* and ready to move ahead wherever God leads me. I ask the Lord to make me *Calm* in difficult situations and help me seek solutions wisely. Finally, I pray that I will always be *Committed* to God.

Growing up, when I went to school, we had prayer and the Pledge of Allegiance to the US flag in school. This is what the United States was founded on by our forefathers and is the one reason we have a democratic society.

This is the prayer I remember saying in school:

The Lord's Prayer
Our Father in heaven
Hallowed be your name,
Your kingdom come,
Your will be done,
On earth as in heaven.
Give us today our daily bread,
And forgive us our debts,
As we forgive our debtors,
And do not subject us to the final test,
But deliver us from the evil one.
Matthew 6:9

There's an old joke that says as long as there are math tests in school, there will always be prayer in school.

Prayer is simple. It is a constant rising of our mind and heart to God. Decide how much you will commit to daily prayer and begin with confidence.

One of the most important elements in a good prayer life is a sense of order and consistency. This means setting a specific time to pray each day. Many people find the morning to be the best, before they begin the rush of the day. But you will have to experiment and find the time that works best for you. It's also helpful to settle on a specific place - a quiet place in your home, your favorite pew at church, or a local park. In addition to order, attitude plays an important role. At the very beginning of your prayer, put your heart and mind in the right place. When doing your daily readings, always have pen or pencil at hand so you can write down how the reading speaks to you.

Remember the saying "it takes 21 days to form a new habit." See if you can pray in the morning and at night for 21 days, and you should be able to form a new habit.

A family should pray for the strength to love one another in good times and bad times, as well as for the strength to meet whatever challenges its family members face. Whether it's a big football game, or a tough exam or an illness or accident – find the time to pray.

I am always very honored when all my brothers and our families get together, and I am asked to pray and bless the food before we eat.

I call this the life's lesson prayer.

The Serenity Prayer

God grant me the serenity
To accept things, I cannot change;
Courage to change the things I can:
And wisdom to know the difference.
Living one day at a time;
Enjoying one moment at a time;
Accepting hardships as the pathway to peace;
Taking, as He did, this sinful world
As it is, not as I would have it;
Trusting that He will make all things right
If I surrender to His Will;
So that I may be reasonable happy in this life
And supremely happy with Him
Forever and ever in the next

Amen.

By Reinhold Niebuhr

Another way to pray and develop a good habit

ABCD Prayer

A – Adoration – Presence of God

B – Blessing – Recognize what God has done

C – Confession – Admit my sins and ask forgiveness

D – Devil – Prayer defeats the devil

Prayer: To you, O Lord, I entrust all my hopes, all my trials and miseries. May all my actions be ordered and disposed according to Your will. As I toil for peace and unity in Your vineyard, make me strong and faithful to praise You ever more. And may nothing ever cloud my conscience or hinder my progress until the day that Jesus comes. Amen.

"Be still and know that I am God" Psalm 46:10

Prayer can be difficult, especially if we think about the mechanics or outcomes. Often, we're anxious about prayer. Does it work? Am I doing it right? Does God answer prayers? How do we know?

One thing we know for certain about prayer: it has been part of the human way of being for as far back as we can look. Human history is saturated with prayer. So is Christian tradition. The gospels give us some sense of the long, sometimes painful hours Jesus spent in prayer. They tell us Jesus exhorted us and taught us to pray.

If you want a change in your life, learn to pray.

You probably have heard that "Silence is Golden." Well, it is especially true when you are in prayer. The next time you are in prayer, listen for the silence.

Listen to sounds of your surroundings.

Listen to the silence of the voice as your body relaxes.

Listen to your mind – your mind will start to wander but listen to your breathing and the silence. If that does not work, say "I lift my eyes to You, Lord" in silence.

If you become content to sit and pray and do not put your hands to the labor of helping your brothers and sisters, prayer becomes self-glorification. We fill ourselves with good ideas, but nothing comes out of them. Remember this: One does not have to say anything, read anything, or pray anything, but just sit before the Lord. Sit Quietly.

> Prayer: Please give me the strength to go on through my life. Give me the wisdom and knowledge to do what is right and *not* wrong. And please, give me the strength to make the right decisions about the things that occur. I know I haven't been making the right decisions, but I'd like to better that. Life has not been easy for me through these times, but I know that you will give me the strength to go on for I do believe in You and all You say and do. Amen.

Let me end with this poem by David M. Romano called:
"When Tomorrow Starts Without Me."
When tomorrow starts without me,
And I'm not there to see,
If the sun should rise and find your eyes
All filled with tears for me;
I wish so much you wouldn't cry
The way you did today,
While thinking of the many things,
We didn't get to say.
I know how much you love me,
As much as I Love You,
And each time you think of me,
I know you'll miss me too;
But when tomorrow starts without me,
Please try to understand,

That an angel came and called my name,
And took me by the hand.

Now take 5 minutes and read Proverbs 16.

Don't read another chapter until you write one thing you have learned from your readings today that will help you become a better person.

_____

_____

_____

_____

_____

_____

_____

_____

_____

_____

_____

_____

_____

_____

_____

_____

_____

_____

_____

_____

Proverbs 16:3 - Entrust your works to the Lord,
and your plans will succeed.

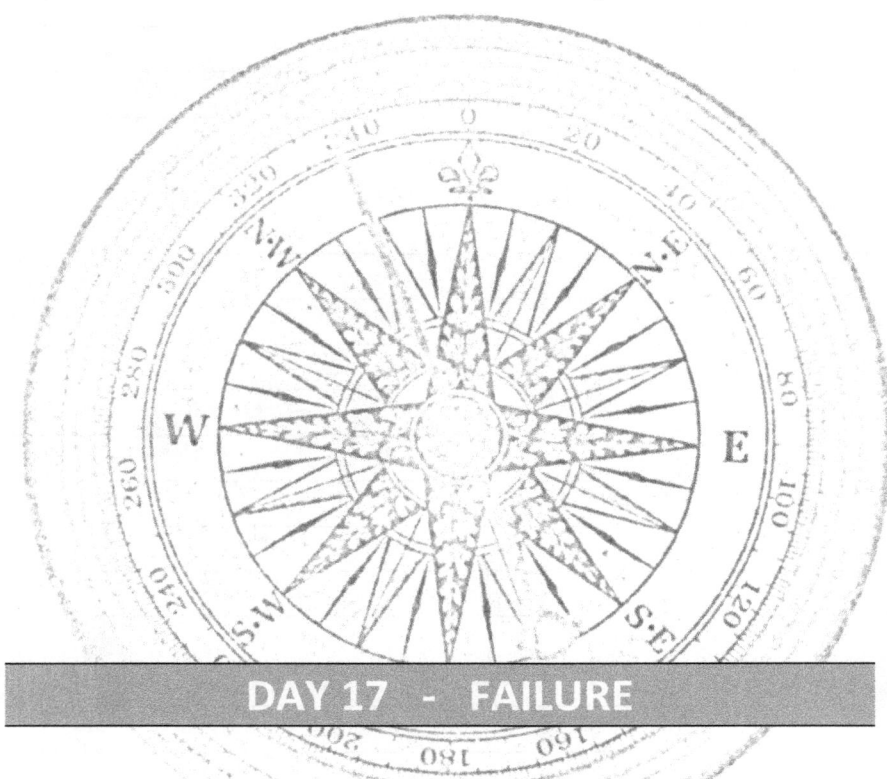

DAY 17 - FAILURE

Deuteronomy 31:8 - It is the Lord who marches before you,
he will be with you and will never fail you or forsake you
So do not fear or be dismayed

Failure is really an opportunity to start over more intelligently. No man ever achieved worthwhile success who did not at one time, or another find himself teetering on the edge of disaster. If you have tried to do something and failed, you are vastly better off than if you had tried to do nothing and succeeded. The person who never makes a mistake must get awfully tired of doing nothing. If you're not making mistakes, you're not risking enough.

There are many ways to become a failure, but never taking a chance is the most successful at being a failure. Let your children fail and through their failures, they will become champions.

One of the greatest problems people have with failure is that they are too quick to judge isolated situations in their lives and label them as failures. Fear is not the feeling of failure. It's the feeling of being judged for your decisions even if the decision was wrong.

You may have failed at something, but you are not a failure. Failure is success if you learn from your failure. You need to quit comparing yourself to others, you need to run your own race. I remember when I ran a lot, I was always trying to improve on how fast I ran a 5K, 10K, 15K or half marathon race. I failed many times trying to get to my goal of running the races under a 6-minute pace, but I finally did it one year, because I never gave up on my goal. Instead, they need to keep the bigger picture in mind. Someone like Tony Gwyn or Babe Ruth (baseball players) didn't look at an out they made as a failure, but they looked at that hit or home run as a bigger success over failure. Perseverance and this perspective on the outcome give them the opportunity for success.

Just look at Abraham Lincoln's road to success through his failures.

Abraham Lincoln:
- Failed in business – 1831
- Defeated for Legislature – 1832
- Again failed in business – 1833
- Elected to Legislature – 1834
- Fiancé' died – 1835
- Defeated for Speaker – 1838
- Defeated for Elector – 1840
- Married but wife a burden – 1842
  and only one of four sons lived past the age of 18
- Defeated for Congress – 1843
- Elected to Congress – 1846
- Defeated for Congress – 1848

- Defeated for Senate – 1855
- Defeated for VP – 1856
- Defeated for Senate – 1858
- Elected President – 1860

> Sometimes the people closes to you can't see the greatest in you.

You never know where success might take you. Failure is not the opposite of success, it's part of success

Fear, I have experienced the unknown in many other areas.

You can pick a fear:
- ✔ Fear of public speaking
- ✔ Fear of marriage
- ✔ Fear of divorce
- ✔ Fear of having children

Same old, same old – we are in a rut and if we do not change our ways, we can't make a difference and fulfill our dreams and goals. Will you stumble and fall? Absolutely, but the key is getting back up. We tumble from the top of the mountain to the valley. It is how long we stay in the valley before we get back on top of the mountain.

Believe it or not, bad things happen to good and bad people alike. Sometimes the people close to you can't see the greatest in you.

God is only heard in time of peaceful silence.

All of us fail. As we drive our car, we all take wrong turns, forget to check the air in the tires or check the oil in the car. The only person who avoids failure altogether is the person who does not own or drive a car. So, the real issue is not whether you're going to fail, it's whether you're going to fail successfully.

I play golf and I enjoy it. I could never have been a professional golfer. But it makes you wonder how they handle failure. They fail or do not win a tournament 90% to 95% of the time. In fact, the best golfer winning percentage as of 2011 was 25.9% by Tiger Woods. A lot of professional golfers never win a tournament, but still try to win. They handle failure on a regular basis, but they are willing to try again and again. Failure is not an option for them.

In Billy Casper 's book "The Big Three and Me Billy" I like what he said:

> Unsuccessful people mainly suffer a mind-deadening thought disease. We call this disease *excusitis*. Every failure has their disease in its advanced form. And most average people have at least a mild case of *excusitis*. You will discover that *excusitis* explains the difference between the person who is going places and the person who is barely holding his own. You will find that the more   successful the individual, the less inclined he is to make excuses. Study the lives of successful people and you will discover this: all the excuses made by the mediocre person could be but aren't made by the successful person.

Excusitis comes in a wide variety of excuses, but the most common ones are: health *excusitis*, intelligence *excusitis*, age *excusitis*, and luck *excusitis*. I want to touch a little on each one and if you see yourself in one or any of these *excusitises*, you may want to change your way of thinking.

1). Health *excusitis* – My health isn't good, and I can't do the things I used to do. I don't feel good in the mornings and I am tired in the afternoon. They might say I have such and such wrong with me. A lot of people are in bad health and they are legitimate, and they should take care of themselves, but there are many who use the health excuse and fail to accept responsibility for getting fit!

There are two ways of handling health problems. One, you can make all the excuses and think something is wrong with you and you never get better. Second, you can tackle your health problems head on and get them fixed. I want to share my experience of health *excusitis*. I was a runner in the Air

Failure is really an opportunity to start over more intelligently.

Force, running between 50 and 70 miles a week. I thought I would never have knee problems or back problems. A few years ago, I was having problems with my knee and the pain became unbearable and I had to do something about it. I finally went to an orthopedic doctor and he recommended I either get shots in the knee or have the knee replaced. I opted to have what they call Rooster Crown injections in my left knee and it came in a series of three separate injections. After the third injection, my knee started feeling better and I was able to start my morning workouts again. Not running, but a combination of cardio and weight training.

Now for my back, it would give me pain in my back and down my leg. After 62 years, I finally went to see a chiropractor to see if he could help. He had x-rays taken and explained to me how my spinal column was out of line and that was causing some of my pain. Luckily, I found the right chiropractor who took the time to explain to me what he could do for me. I was not sure after the first couple of sessions, but now after a few months I can see a major difference with my back and the pain has almost gone away. It is amazing when you take care of yourself and get medical attention how much better you can feel.

2). The Intelligence *excusitis* is the one excuse that most people do not say but are always thinking about. They wish that they were smarter. We all see ourselves short on intelligence. Most of the time you don't want to challenge yourself with any new work or challenges. We are satisfied with what we do and what we have. You need to challenge yourself and believe you can tackle the challenge. A positive, optimistic, and cooperative attitude will give a person a better chance to succeed and tackle those challenges. A person who is negative, pessimistic, and uncooperative with a higher intelligence will not succeed as well as the positive person with lower intelligence.

I was always told growing up that my brothers and I would not make anything of ourselves. We grew up in the projects and did not have a lot to speak of growing up. It was day to day for our family most of the time. I started working as soon as I could. By the time I was a senior in high school, I had bought my first new car on my own. It was a 1968 Chevy Malibu. Everyone at the high school did not know what to think. They thought I was into drugs. They were so wrong, and I can honestly say I have never taken drugs. I worked at a grocery store and a gas station while I was going to high school and I made good money for my age and I also played football and baseball. Let me tell you a little bit more. I went into the Air Force six months after I graduated from high school and five years later, I got out to finish college through the AFROTC program and was commissioned an officer in the USAF where I had a very successful twenty-one-year career. I also graduated as a distinguished graduate through the AFROTC program. I tell you this so you can understand I was not the smartest person, but a very positive, hard working person. Knowledge is powerful if you use it. Never underestimate yourself and always understand that there are other intelligent people.

3). The third excuse people use is age, I am too old, I can't do that, or I am too young, I can't do that either. Is age a factor? Yes, for a lot of people. They let their age get to them. Curing yourself of the age *excusitis* will open many doors for you once you believe. You are only as old as you think you are and as you feel. Almost everyone is very productive into their 70's. Now let's look at the other side of the age factor. I am too young – I can't supervise people older than me. I learned in the military to be a supervisor at a very young age. Did I believe I could supervise? Yes, I did. Did I have problems and a big learning curve? You bet. The military puts you in positions to learn and to grow. As a Second Lieutenant (age 26) I had a lot to learn about being a supervisor, but also a leader. Most of the enlisted personnel were in their late 30's and 40's, and you learn quickly to not worry about the age factor. Demonstrate that you have the ability and positive attitude and your age will not be a factor and you will earn their respect.

4). The fourth excuse people use is that they are not lucky. There is hardly a day that goes by that someone doesn't blame their problems on "bad luck." And it is rare that you do not hear someone attribute another person's success to "good luck."

I have been on many interview panels over the years for jobs under my responsibility. It has been interesting to hear people talk about "why" they did not get selected for a job. It ranges from the person who was selected was lucky, they were a brown noser, had an in with the boss, went to lunch with the boss, everything but the truth. The truth is that the person selected for the job was the better qualified and worked harder than the other candidates.

Let me ask you – why do you use the luck *excusitis*? So, do you want to get rid of using luck as an excuse? Here are a couple of things you can work on to eliminate luck *excusitis*. First, don't waste time thinking that luck has anything to do with success. Success comes from doing things that others will not do. So, work on developing the qualities you need to get promoted to the next level in your career. Second, admit that good luck and bad luck have nothing to do with you being successful.

What if on our foreheads we had neon signs saying how we feel or our hidden secrets and failures. We don't have to be perfect, but we need to admit failures and shortcomings. Be careful who you admit them to - your significant other, your pastor, good friend, or your parents. Don't judge others.

But, the expression "to pay the price" evokes other scenarios. How many athletes, artists, and researchers have accepted to pay the price of victory, a masterpiece, or a discovery? How many people have paid the price for their own desires?

Now take 5 minutes and read Proverbs 17.

Don't read another chapter until you write one thing you have learned from your readings today that will help you become a better person.

Proverbs 17:2 - An intelligent servant will rule over a
worthless son, and will share the inheritance
with the brothers.

DAY 18 - JEALOUSY

*James 3:14 - But if you have bitter jealousy and selfish
ambition in your hearts, do not boast and
be false to the truth.*

Are you jealous or envious of others who you think are being treated better than you with jobs and promotions? It is envy that destroys generosity. Do you worry about what people think about you? If you do, then you need to worry about something else. As you get older your feelings and opinions of what others think does not affect you as much as it did when you were younger.

If you're looking for someone to blame, just look in the mirror.

Have you heard the expression "keeping up with the Jones'?" If you are jealous about what other people have or own, like a new house or car, then you go out and buy a new house or car you just proved that you are jealous of what others have.

There is no challenge that cannot be met and dreams that cannot be achieved.

You may think it's too late – your dreams are too big, your obstacles too difficult. If you're going to become the winner you were created to be, you need to have a boldness. The second quality of a winner is that you run your race the way you want to run it.

Everyone has opinions. If you try to keep everyone happy the one person who will not be happy is, you. Some people will not be able to handle your success. If you did the same job, lived in the same place and never improved yourself, they would have no problem with you. But as you succeed, some of your family, friends, and co-workers will be jealous. Some will find fault in how you succeeded. You will be surprised by what they will say about you to discredit you. But you have to realize that they are not *jealous* of you but upset with themselves because they have not succeeded. Learn to not take it personally. It is hard to do, but you can do it. We are all *jealous* of something someone has done but be a better person and get over your jealousy as quickly as possible. But remember someone is always going to talk about you and the best advice I can give you is that you can only control yourself.

> If you're looking for someone to blame, just look in the mirror.

What I am saying is almost everyone feels that their own opinions are good ones. Otherwise, they wouldn't be sharing them with you. One of the destructive things that many of us do, however, is compare someone else's opinion to our own. And, when it doesn't fall in line with our belief, we either dismiss it or find fault with it. We feel smug – the other person feels diminished – and we learn nothing.

Almost every opinion has some merit especially if we are looking for merit rather than looking for errors. The next time someone offers you an opinion, rather than judge or criticize it, see if you can find a grain of truth in what the person is saying. If you think about it, when you judge someone else or their opinion, it really doesn't say anything about the other person, but it says quite a bit about your need to be judgmental.

When we judge or criticize another person, it says nothing about that person; it only says something about our own need to be critical. Being critical not only solves nothing, it contributes to the anger and distrust in our world. After all, none of us likes to be criticized. Our reaction to criticism is usually to become defensive and/or withdrawn.

I have been in management for many years. The one thing I have learned about providing criticism to someone is to give them positive feedback first, then provide the criticism, and lastly give them another positive feedback. I call this the peanut butter and jelly approach. I have never had someone say "thank you so much for pointing out my flaws. I really appreciate it." But you should be honest with the people who work for you if you are providing their performance evaluations.

No matter what you say, you will never please everybody. They will always find fault with something you have done to succeed.

Have you noticed how young children get jealous of their siblings when they can do something better than the younger sibling? Michele has two grandchildren 9 and 7 years old. The 9-year-old is a boy and the 7-year-old is a girl. The girl tries to outdo her brother all the time. Just the other day, the boy learned to ride his bike without training wheels. The sister was so jealous that she started crying because her brother was able to do something she couldn't do at the time. Her grandmother had to calm her down by telling her that she would work with her the next time she visited and help her ride without the training wheels. Michele was able to calm her down and make her realize that she was younger and couldn't do everything that her big brother could do.

At some point you are going to be jealous of something or someone. The key is not to let that jealousy consume you and create a bad attitude. Get over it quickly!

Now take 5 minutes and read Proverbs 18.

Don't read another chapter until you write one thing you have learned from your readings today that will help you become a better person.

_____

_____

_____

_____

_____

_____

_____

_____

_____

_____

_____

_____

_____

_____

_____

_____

_____

_____

_____

_____

_____

_____

_____

_____

_____

_____

_____

*Proverbs 18:2 - The fool takes no delight in understanding,
but rather in displaying what he thinks.*

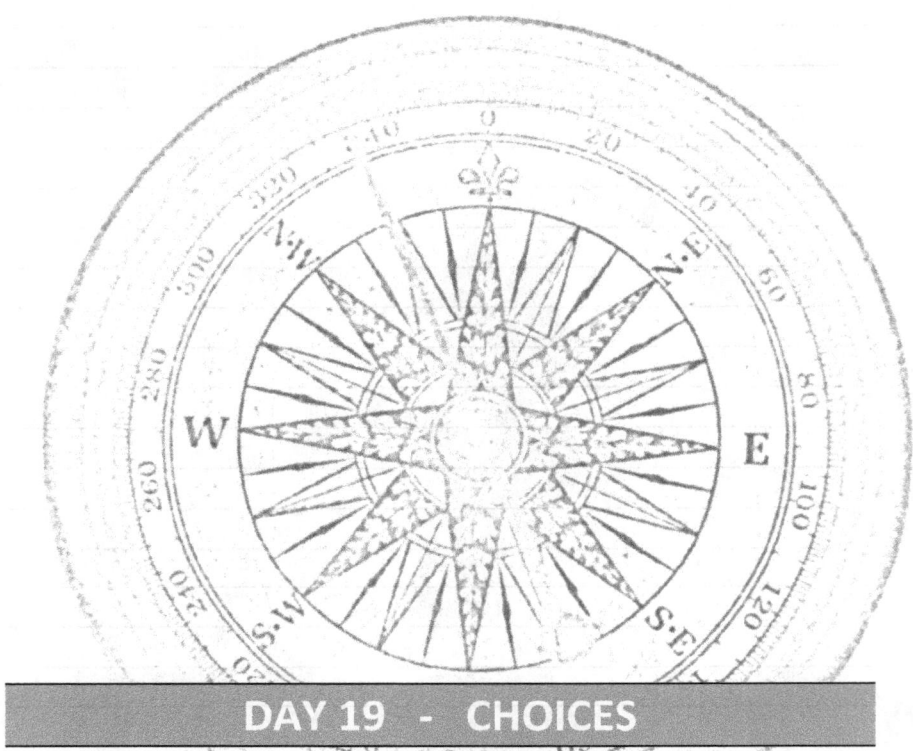

DAY 19 - CHOICES

Ecclesiastes 3:1-2 - There is an appointed time for every-thing, and a time for every affair under the heavens. A time to be born and a time to die, a time to plant, and a time to uproot the plant.

Song: *Beautiful* by Carole King – this song clearly makes the point that you have a choice to wake up every morning with a smile on your face.

"All blame is a waste of time. No matter how much fault you find with another, and regardless of how much you blame him, it will not change you. The only thing blame does is to keep the focus off you when you are looking for extreme reasons to explain your un-happiness or frustration. You may succeed in making another feel guilty about something by blaming him, but you won't succeed in change, whatever it is about you that is making you unhappy."
Wayne Dyer

A quote that my daughter Crystal posted on Reflection (4/23/14)

> *Action is the only way anything ever gets done. Sitting around and waiting for life to happen to you will only guarantee one thing – that you're not going to end up with a life you love. By waiting, you can react to what's tossed your way and nothing more. It's easy to take a passive approach to life without taking chances. It's easy to fall into a rut and do the same things, the same way, all the time. Change is what's hard, but it's change that will reveal all the wonders that life has to offer. You can break out of your set ways by taking action. Try doing the same thing a different way. Jump in with both feet and learn something new. Ask a friend to teach you a skill they're good at. Grow as a person and your world will grow with you.*

"When you stand still you reject the struggle and you refuse to change and grow. Ultimately, you reject fulfillment, happiness, the dance for joy and everything else that is eternally good."
Matthew Kelly

I had written the following down some years back, not sure where it came from, but it is so true.

<u>Weak</u> is he who permits his
<u>Thoughts</u> to control his actions.
<u>Strong</u> is he who forces his
<u>Actions</u> to control his thoughts!

The Blame Meter: One of the great inventions of all time would be a blame meter. Imagine a few wires you hook up to your wrist and every time you blame your misfortunes on something or someone, it registers on the blame meter. In fact, it registers with a warning message that says in a robotic voice. "Warning! You are blaming someone else or circumstances for your problems! You are in danger of self-destructing! Cease your blaming immediately!"

Maybe after a while we would stop blaming circumstances and people and start taking responsibility! In today's downsized and stressful workplace, it is easier than ever to feel unappreciated and overworked. Add family and financial pressures and it is easy to see why some very positive employees would turn to the "blame game."

What are the dangers of "blaming?" If we do it enough, we actually start to believe we are right! At that point, reality becomes distorted and any hope of success, much less happiness becomes a distant dream. Sure, you will still get through life, but you will lose any chance of reaching your "giant dreams," the ones that inspire the soul. "My boss is the problem; he/she gives me very little support."

"If my wife/husband would just stop nagging me!" "It's not my fault my sales are down; the company doesn't do any advertising!" The list goes on endlessly for the people who would rather "excuse their lives away."

Actually, we do have a "blame meter." It is called reality. Somewhere deep in the recesses of our mind, we know that ultimately, we are responsible for our own success or failure in any given circumstance. If we are determined to reach our goals and dreams, taking responsibility for the reality of our choices (to blame or not to blame), is a key step in the truly successful life.

The great writer, George Bernard Shaw wrote, "People are always blaming their circumstances for what they are. I don't believe in circumstances. The people who get on in this world are the people who get up and look for the circumstances they want, and, if they can't find them, they make them."

What a powerful statement! Put simply, if you spend time shaping your destiny instead of letting the world shape it for you, the world's richest come to you in abundance.

Turn your blame meter on full power, determine to shape your reality as you would like it to be and there is no limit to what you can accomplish! When we stop blaming circumstances and people for our limitations, we elevate ourselves above the level of ordinary into the realm of champions. Once you stop blaming, action takes over your daily life. Action leads to a positive self-image, self-image leads to positive attitude, a positive attitude leads to unlimited energy and purpose, transforming your world above the ordinary life that most people resign themselves to live.

Live to win!

 Remember - when you blame someone for something, you are pointing one finger at them and three fingers are pointing back at you.

I like this quote I saw on a poster:
"Choice, not chance, determines one's destiny."

Choices, choices, choices. Life is full of choices and you make over 2,500 choices everyday: do you want vanilla, butter pecan or rocky road ice cream or do I want a peanut butter and jelly sandwich. These, and others like them, are choices of little consequence in the whole scheme of things.

Do you sometimes feel other people's choices affect you more than your own? Have you made big decisions in the past but always wound up with smaller results? Are you able to see where your current choices are taking you? Would you like to start making better choices that are realistic today?

We are what we choose. Some of our choices are important to daily life but have no moral impact. Nearly everyone has made wrong choices about something. That is human nature, the key is deciding to change your choice and choose to go another direction, but do not make a quick choice, think about it and think about the results. When you make a choice, you are taking responsibility for that decision. Sometimes circumstances my leave you with only a little control over that circumstance. Your attitude will help you, by focusing on what you can control and not worry about what you cannot control.

How important are the choices we make? To make decisions that last, you must become more aware of your options and their consequences. One of the most important factors in making wise decisions is good information. If you were deciding to change jobs, what would determine your choice? Would it be more money, a better job, a better boss, better location, and better opportunities for future job promotions? You will need to gather all this kind of information before you make that final decision.

Some suggest those who make decisions should use both the head and the heart - but emotions can deceive and lead **you** to wrong decisions. The next time you need to make a decision, use your head and your heart.

The first example of "passing the buck" was when Adam would not accept responsibility for his actions and blames Eve for eating fruit from the forbidden tree. Eve in turn blames the serpent and here is where "passing the buck" really started.

When you blame and criticize others, that means you are avoiding some truth about yourself. People are responsible for their choices and for their actions. Our decisions are complicated by social and emotional situations and by established structures and patterns, but they are our responsibility.

Train a child to make right choices – right from wrong. You do this over and over and over again. It is just like the Navy Seals – they train over and over on all situations, preparing themselves so when the situation comes up, they are well prepared to make the right choices.

Right Decisions – choices we make. We will make some right choices and some wrong choices. In practice, most people look closer to get their guidance and seek it first from people they know like relatives, friends, co-workers, members of the clergy, business associates and others. The people we take guidance from directly determine the choices we make, and this is where we end up in life.

Life is too short to wake up one morning with regrets

People have two centers of decision-making in their lives. The first is the head, the seat of reason and logic. When faced with a decision, head-thinkers allow the mind to guide them. Others think from the heart, the seat of emotion and feeling. When faced with a decision, heart-thinkers do what feels right and what creates the least conflict within their emotions.

Courage – we need the intestinal fortitude to keep doing what needs to be done to make progress. The first step in many ways is the most difficult of all. I was always wondering if I would ever ask a girl out for a date in high school. At some point we all face mountains in life - situations that seem beyond our coping abilities.

Life is too short to wake up in the morning with regrets. So, love the ones who treat you right, forget the ones who don't remember that everything happens for a reason. If you get a chance, take it, if it changes your life then let it. No one said it would be easy, they just promised it would be worth it.

Perhaps each of us can recall moments when others who have been responsible for us or responsible to make us responsible for ourselves. We experienced that sense of joy that comes with being allowed to do something on one's own for the first time; for example, a great commission, the relaying of an important message, undertaking a special task, or simply being old enough to venture out on your own. Yes, great things happen when the responsibility of faith takes root, but the responsibility that has been handed over to us as we know all too well, can be frightening.

A week before my daughter's wedding in September, I realized I needed to make a decision about renting a tent for the wedding in case it rained since it had been raining more often that year than in the past. She had planned an outdoor wedding at a very nice private setting. I wanted to take a chance to see if the forecast predicted rain or not before paying $1,500.00 for a tent. I rented the tent. It rained the week and days before the wedding, but it was cloudy on the wedding day but no rain. Sometimes, you have to make decisions based on the possibility that something may happen, like it may rain and ruin the wedding. Decisions are not hard to make when you have all the facts, but sometimes you must make decisions without all the facts or assumptions.

Also, one year we went to a football game between Florida and Idaho. It had been sunny all day, but at 7pm, right before game time, it started to get dark and cloudy. Even though we thought the clouds were pretty far away, we decided to go inside the stadium. At 6:30pm there were lightning strikes, and the game was suspended until the lightning stopped. It started raining really hard with thunder and lightning, but soon it appeared that the lightning was out of the area and so they kicked off. Florida ran the ball back 64 yards to the 14. Then it started raining very hard again, and once more the game was suspended. This went on for some time until the game was finally cancelled around 10:30pm.

Some things can control you or you become addicted to something and before you can overcome the addiction, it has an iron clad grip on every ounce of your body. You must make a decision to overcome it. It will be hard at first, but it is worth it, as long as you have hope and friends who stick by you, then your life can change, and you can have control of it. The support system of friends and your hope will keep you on the right path to overcome the addiction.

You've just got to be kidding me. Sometimes we have to make decisions for our family, life and careers. I know when I made the decision to take the job in Hernando County, Florida, it was a difficult one for my family. I was looking at the challenge and opportunity to make some changes. It was a good decision as far as the job opportunity and promotions, but not for the family overall.

We always ask ourselves – Why me? Why now? Why at all?

I was very content with my current job situation. But in my walk of faith I have determined that God always marks our paths with boulders and breadcrumbs. The boulders are the huge things, the unstoppable signs of God's direction. We often see the breadcrumbs or what I have termed "God's silent whispers" only in hindsight. God whispers to us in many ways, but we don't always listen. But, through prayer He whispers every minute of every day. I was driving to work one day after I had decided to change jobs. Everyone wondered why I made the decision to change jobs. On the side of a moving truck were the words: "You have made the right decision." That was the confirmation I needed to know that my faith and belief was confirmed in some way.

At every intersection of our daily lives, you and I are presented with some kind of choice. In a situation, a circumstance, encounter with another person, maybe someone you don't want to see. You ask yourself, am I going to be a blessing or a curse? Another way to look at it is, am I going to be the light in the dark tunnel, or I am going to curse the darkness and be the dark side.

Well, I have a confession to make, sometimes I make the wrong response virtually every day and my guess is, so do you. Why? Because we don't live in a perfect world and we are not perfect. Not everyone is nice to us all the time. Let's face it, we are all often hurt by people who are inconsiderate, demanding, unreasonable, undependable, arrogant, critical, dishonest and even downright nasty.

And sometimes life seems to kick us in the teeth, through events, situations and circumstances, that we can't control and that leaves us disappointed, frustrated, angry and depressed. How do we tend to react? With anger, resentment, bitterness, judgment and a bunch of other not so pleasant thoughts.

The next time this happens, how about smiling or laughing at the whole situation. That smile will change your outlook/attitude and maybe someone else's.

It's very helpful to remind yourself that your life isn't your enemy, but your thinking can be. While you're at it, remind yourself of the tremendous power of your thinking, that your world is shaped by those thoughts you choose to focus on the most.

Quality
is never an accident;
it is always the result

of high intentions,
sincere effort,
intelligent direction
and skillful
execution; it
represents the wise
choice of many
alternatives

Now take 5 minutes and read Proverbs 19.

Don't read another chapter until you write one thing you have learned from your readings today that will help you become a better person.

_____

_____

_____

_____

_____

_____

_____

_____

_____

_____

_____

_____

_____

_____

_____

_____

_____

_____

Proverbs 19:1 - Better a poor man who walks in his integrity than he who is crooked in his ways and rich.

DAY 20 - STRESS/WORRY

Matthew 6:34 - Do not worry about tomorrow, for tomorrow will worry about itself. Each day has enough trouble of its own.

Song: *Three Little Birds* by Bob Marley

People can't be happy until they've learned to use what they have and not worry over what they don't have. Happiness never comes to those who fail to appreciate what they already have. Most people make the mistake of looking too far ahead for things close by. Make the most of what you have, no matter the circumstances. If you wait for perfect conditions, you'll never get anything done! We all must row with the oars we've been given. You can never get much of anything done unless you go ahead and do it before you are ready. No one ever made a success of anything by waiting around until all conditions were "just right." Don't waste time in doubts and fears about what you don't have; take time for yourself in the task before you, knowing the right performance of this hour's duties will be the best preparation for the hours or years that follow.

You must make time for yourself to relax.

How many times at work do you see someone worrying about their co-worker who is late for work every morning or late coming back from lunch? You would be better off worrying about what you can do instead of worrying about your co-worker. Management should take care of your co-worker if they thought it was important or if they didn't already know why the person was late.

We are busy people. We try to fit everything in a day. You work all day and then you drive home in the traffic to spend time with your spouse and/or children. You might have to drive your children to a practice or event of some kind. We are people who bring work home every night in hopes we will still have time to do other things in our life. You are not satisfied to be a passive observer of life, and so you have immersed yourselves in life's activities and responsibilities. We are busy people, but you must make time for yourself and relax. If not, worry and stress will work against you.

How to help your stress/worry. Making people laugh should be everyone's **#1** goal each day. Laughter is the shock absorber of life's hard knocks. It is internal jogging. Experts say that laughter helps control pain in four ways; 1) by distracting attention, 2) by reducing tension, 3) by changing expectations, and 4) by increasing the production of endorphins – the body's natural pain killers.

By laughing we are not denying that we have problems. We laugh to make sure the problems don't overwhelm us. There is a close connection between laughing and crying. Sometimes we laugh so hard we start crying. Does laughing make you feel better? I believe that 99.9% of people who laugh feel a lot better after they have had a good laugh.

Married Life: A husband once said that he and his wife were inseparable. In fact, he said "last week it took two policemen and their dog to separate them."

There are many stressful situations in life:
Raising Children
Politics and Government
The Legal System
The Work Place
The Aging Process
Organized Religion

Stress has been controlling Americans more than people in other countries. We are always in a hurry - fast food, fast lane, fast cars and hurry up for the weekend.

We are always in a hurry. This is the beginning of a new day. God has given us this new day to use as we will. We can waste it or use it for good. What you do today is important because you're exchanging a day of your life for it. When tomorrow comes this day will be gone forever, leaving in its place something we have traded for it. We want it to be **a** gain not **a** loss, good not evil, success not failure, so we won't regret the price we paid for it. At work we all have heard people say they wish they could slow down. Slowing down is something we must do no matter what our age. I know you have heard the phrase "Stop and smell the roses." We do need to slow down and really stop and smell the roses every chance we can.

> Don't ruin a good day today by thinking about a bad day yesterday.

Not everyone gets stressed out when someone pulls in front of them when they are driving. But when you find out they are on their cell phone talking or texting you can really get stressed out. It is almost like most people who are on their phones lose their brain and have no clue what they are doing while they are driving.

If you are complaining to yourself, to others or to God that you are stressed out, then you basically have two choices: 1) You could lighten your load and stop complaining, or 2) You could stop complaining totally. To a great extent, burnout is a state of mind. A good friend of mine used to make himself miserable constantly by telling me how tired he was and how busy he was at work. He also made everyone around him miserable, too. He may or may not have been too busy; some thought he made himself too busy by the way he did his work. But one thing is clear; his preoccupation with his stress levels did nothing to alleviate the problem.

Maybe money is your greatest source of stress and it usually is #1 reason; it fits right in with the philosophy of learning to be less worried, stressed, annoyed and irritated. You can't (and probably don't want to) avoid the issues surrounding money, but you can learn to take it more in stride. And when you do, your entire life will become more relaxed and peaceful.

Believe it or not, your attitude makes a big difference on your stress level. If you think you are really busy and don't have any time to do things, then you are stressed out. If you are able to control your attitude and look at things from a different perspective, you can reduce your stress level.

Time takes no vacation, nor is it put in neutral. So, don't worry! Time will heal all wounds.

Don't ruin a good day by thinking about a BAD yesterday.

Now take 5 minutes and read Proverbs 20.

Don't read another chapter until you write one thing you have learned from your readings today that will help you become a better person.

_____
_____
_____
_____
_____
_____
_____
_____
_____
_____

_____

_____

_____

_____

_____

_____

_____

_____

_____

_____

_____

_____

_____

_____

_____

_____

_____

_____

_____

_____

_____

_____

_____

_____

*Proverbs 20:3 - A person gains honor by avoiding strife,
while every fool starts a quarrel.*

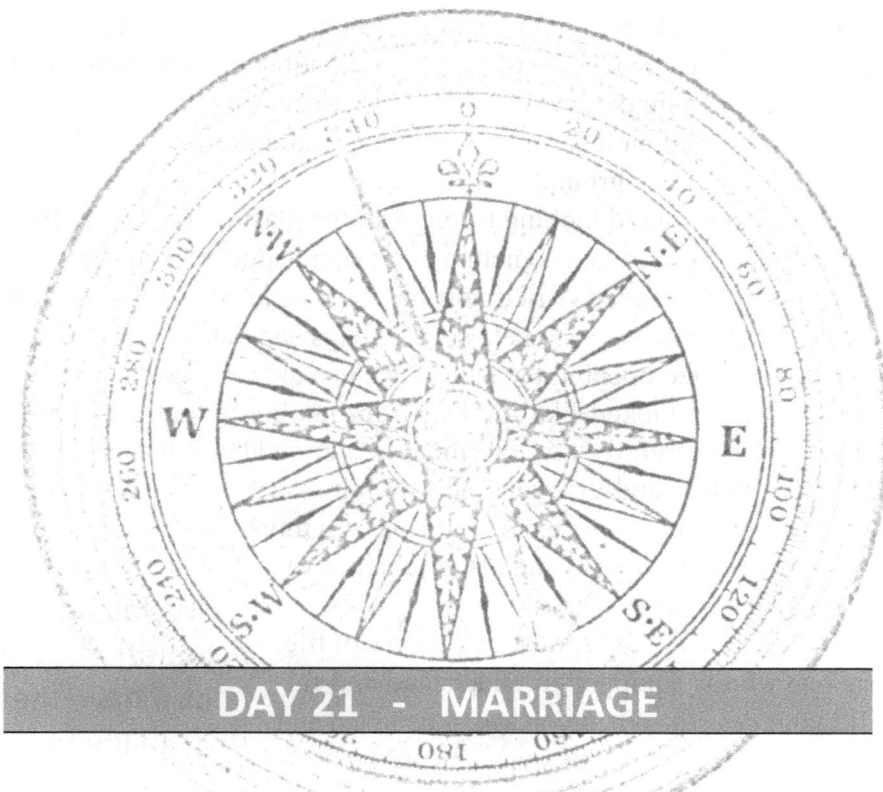

DAY 21 - MARRIAGE

Ephesians 5:31-33 - A man shall leave his father and mother
and be joined to his wife, and the two
shall become one flesh.

I remember a story that was told at church one Sunday. This man had lost his wedding ring and he knew he had put it on the kitchen counter when he went to bed that night. He looked everywhere for it and finally realized that the only place it could be was in the trash can next to the counter. The cat always played with things on the counter. But, today was trash day and his wife took out the trash when she left for work. He went outside to get the trash bag from the curb, but the trash had already been picked up.

The trash substation was about 2 miles from his house, so he jumped in the car and drove very quickly to the substation. He told the attendant at the substation his situation. The attendant said the truck that picked up from the man's street had not been there yet, so he waited. The attendant was very understanding and said that when the truck came in, they would put all the trash from the truck in one area. About an hour later, the truck finally came in and the trash was dumped out on the ground.

The man started looking through all the plastic bags and at first it was very difficult, but something amazing happened and the truck driver and the loader started sorting the plastic bags for him and more drivers came over to help sort the bags and once the bags were sorted he started opening the bags in a clean area. He got to one bag and he said it looked like the bag from his house and it was. He looked very carefully through the bag and suddenly he found the ring in the bag and everyone around him started clapping and of course there were some tears. The ring was more than a ring, it was the symbol of the man's and his wife's love for each other.

You look to your spouse as a source of life, as one who is equipped to understand and fulfill your desires. When you ask to be loved and respected you want your spouse to offer to give you what you long for so you can experience satisfaction. When your spouse does not give you what you have requested, you are unfulfilled and disappointed. Since you believe that what your heart craves can be found in your marriage, you are hurt and troubled when your desire isn't fulfilled. When you are not offered what you long to receive, you feel emptiness, pain, or dissatisfaction.

> We all have limitations; we also have the ability to adapt.

Marriage is Bigger Than You! The meaning of marriage transcends what you get out of it, whether you are happy or sad, content or discontent. Many people say they remain in difficult marriages because they made a vow or entered into a covenant relationship. This implies that the reason for staying in a marriage is not the value of marriage but the value of a commitment or vow. Does a person refuse to have an affair simply because he or she promised faithfulness to a spouse? If that is the primary reason, then the spouse is likely to feel very proud of their choice to remain faithful. But, if the partner believes in the sacredness of sexual intimacy and celebration with the one with whom he or she has become one flesh before God, having sex with another person will not make sense. A promise may serve as a reminder, but **it** is not a basis for marital faithfulness.

Difficult Times: Is your marriage difficult and causing you pain because you have communication problems and fight all the time? Are things not working because you don't spend enough time together? Is the basic problem in your marriage that your spouse had an affair or looks at pornography? Does your spouse never forget anything that you ever did wrong? Or do you think you lack a common vision and fail to support each other in your dreams? Is it a lack of forgiveness or prayer? Or is it a conflict with the in-laws? There is an easy answer. So, you think the problem is your spouse! *WRONG.* There are many ways to define marital problems and diagnose difficulties in a marriage. *HINT:* the problem isn't your spouse. It's something else or you! We all have limitations, limited capacities; limited capacity for understanding, emotional expression or growth. You have to have the ability to adapt.

Take 5 minutes and write down strengths you see in your spouse. They will appreciate it, but more importantly you will appreciate what they do.

	HUSBAND		WIFE
H	– Honest		
U	– Understanding	W	– Warm Hearted
S	– Strong	I	– Intuitive
B	– Big Hearted	F	– Faithful
A	– Affectionate	E	– Empathetic &
N	– Needed		Emotional
D	– Dependable		

Feelings change because we are human beings. Any marriage or relationship lasting more than a few months has good and bad times. Everything is easy when you are enthusiastic and have high energy. Mature, deeply loving relationships develop stronger only after the first heated argument days have passed. Sometimes you may feel like that is all you do. But if you learn from those days, your relationship will become stronger. However, many of us know people who go from relationship to relationship, breaking up as soon as the newness begins to wear off.

> Do you want me to listen or to help solve the problem?

Three important sayings you need to use in your marriage:

May I …

Thank You …

I Am Sorry …

Men – don't try to solve your wife's problems, but ask her this question: "Do you want me to listen or to help solve the problem?"

Three things to greatly increase the odds for a successful marriage:
1. Pray together – aloud daily
2. Read your bible together – daily
3. Attend church services together – regularly every week

Companionship

Lonely – Love

Feeling alone and lonely, heightens our fears of inadequacy. Loneliness pushes you to behavior that even compounds the loneliness. In our alienation from others, paranoia grips us. When this happens, we search to feel a connection with someone, and this usually ends up being with another lonely person. Usually when two lonely people get together, they do not look at themselves but start gossiping about others.

We all need a sense of belonging, belonging to your workplace, belonging to your neighborhood, belonging to the group we call friends and belonging to our family. Knowing that we belong fosters the inner peace that accompanies security, well-being and the fears of loneliness are melted away.

We need to be attentive to our judgments of others, be they verbalized in gossip or only in our silence. These judgments act as a barometer of our self-image and in our security in knowing we belong; it relieves us from the need to judge others unfairly. Real closeness will come when we talk about ourselves rather than talk about others.

True happiness, however, does not come from the pleasures of this world, nor by the accumulation of wealth. It comes from you not feeling alone and that you have a sense of belonging.

Humans and Animals

Have you ever noticed how animals show their love, especially if you have been gone for a period of time? They need companionship also. My cat, Flash, is a good example. There was a period of time when I was gone during the week and only home on the weekends. When I came home, she was all over me!

Just as food is required for human life, so are companions. Companions nourish our heart, mind, soul, and body. Perhaps the most touching stories in the bible are about companionship – the Last Supper, the sharing of the loaves and fish.

Sometimes we are disappointed by others who are our companions, but if they are truly faithful companions then they will come back stronger.

> ## Pope Francis Urges Couples to Raise Kids, Not Cats and Dogs
>
> Pope Francis said that staying childless will ultimately bring married couples nothing but "the bitterness of loneliness."
>
> Pope Francis had a message for married couples on Monday: four legged friends don't offer the same opportunities for love and godliness as raising a child.

The Pope addressed a group of 15 couples that have been married between 25 and 60 years during daily Mass on Monday, held in the chapel of the Santa Maria residence in the Vatican. The Pope stressed the importance of three qualities in a successful Christian marriage – faithfulness, perseverance and fruitfulness – during his remarks, according to Vatican Radio.

But the Pope also counseled childless couples to be fruitful and multiply, and not spend time raising pets when they could be raising children. Mentioning the "culture of well-being," similar to one mentioned in the 2013 TIME cover story "The Childfree Life," Pope Francis said that while a childless life offers better vacation opportunities, it will end in solitude: This culture of well-being from 10 years ago convinced us: It's better not to have children! It's better! You can go explore the world, go on holiday, you can have a villa in the countryside, you can be carefree... it might be better – more comfortable – to have a dog, two cats, and the love goes to the two cats and the dog. Is this true or is this not? Have you seen it? Then, in the end this marriage comes to old age in solitude, with the bitterness of loneliness. It is not fruitful; it does not do what Jesus does with his Church: He makes His church fruitful.

In other words, all the effort you spend caring for your furry friends would be of better use if Fido or Fifi were children.

(Excerpt from St. Peter Catholic Church Bulletin
June 15, 2014)

Now take 5 minutes and read Proverbs 21.

Don't read another chapter until you write one thing you have learned from your readings today that will help you become a better person.

_Proverbs 21:23 - He who guards his mouth and
his tongue keeps himself from trouble._

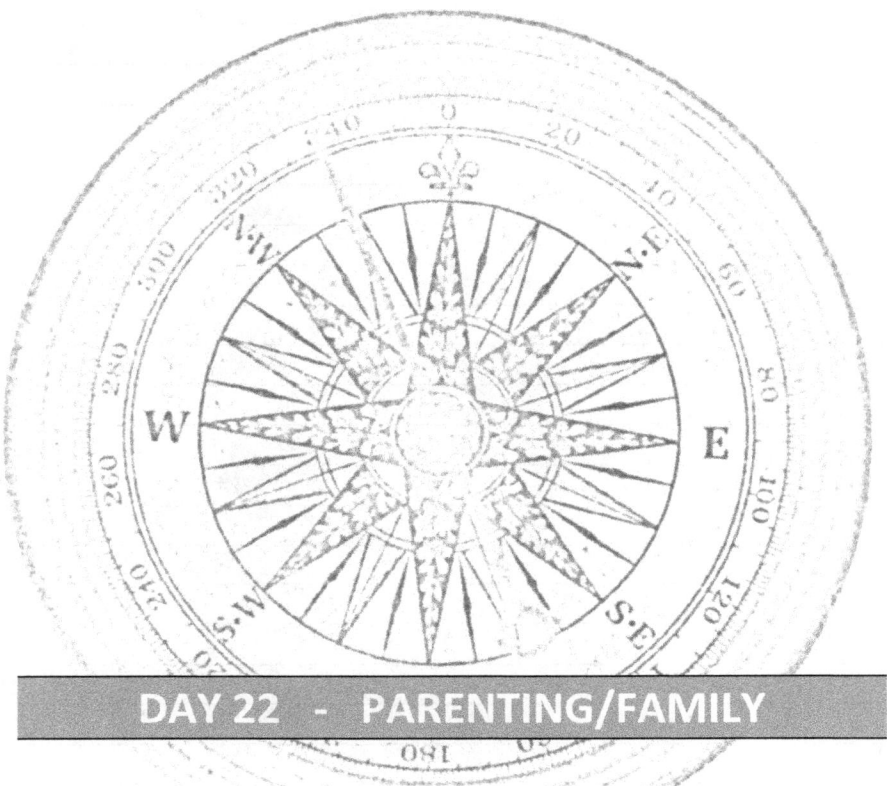

DAY 22 - PARENTING/FAMILY

Ephesians 6:1-2 - Children obey your parents in the Lord for it is right. "Honor your father and mother" – which is the first commandment with a promise.

God is not described as knowing everything beforehand. For example, he discovers the disobedience of Adam and Eve eating fruit from the forbidden tree in the Garden of Eden, which opened Adam's and Eve's eyes to their nakedness. We are reminded of a parent figuring out that their children have been in the cookie jar because they have chocolate all over their faces.

Our attitude and growth never stop. Our attitudes are formed by our experiences and how we choose to react to them. Your surrounding conditions as you grow up and the people who you surround yourself with, will have a major impact on your positive and negative outlook on life.

Did you make time for your children? If so you might hear these words: You made time to play games with me, listened to my stories, and took pride in my accomplishments. You still have a way of making me feel good about myself whenever I talk to you.

Unconditional Love/Discipline:
This is called agape love. I was at a religious retreat when I first heard the definition of agape love.

When you are going through hard times discipline makes you grow stronger. Just because you discipline someone does not mean you do not love them. Discipline shows the unconditional love for that person.

Discipline:
There are many ways you can discipline your children. Each child needs to be disciplined in a way that corrects the unwanted behavior you want to change. I remember when I was growing up the principals and coaches of the public schools were able to discipline us without recourse. That is not so at these times.

The breakdown of the family unit is the single deepest ethical and moral challenge to families today. When it comes to teaching values, actions always speak louder than words. They need to see the value lived out by you. Always take time to sit and talk to your kids. Don't be afraid to say what you feel. Always strive to teach your kids to love and respect themselves. A healthy love and respect for themselves is incredibly important for any kid. Being a parent is a tough job. Most of us, if not all of us, were never taught to be parents. So, we can't help but disappoint ourselves sometimes!

Families were the building blocks of all great societies, but that is not true anymore. People and families live in the midst of societies and cultures. Our present culture does not lend itself to families.

Communicating your values has never been more important than it is today. And the good news is all begins and ends with you. When all is said and done, parents have more influence over instilling values in their kids that any other factors.

Yes, some others may influence your kids, but you are the "value makers."

Kids get their sense of what's right and wrong from people they love and respect. No one has more influence over teaching values than you do. Your input can make all the difference.

When it comes to teaching values, actions *always* speak louder than words. Kids today have a "show me mentality." They need to see the values lived out by you. Respect for life, respect for other people, honesty, integrity - kids get these from *watching you*. The old saying has never been truer; children do learn what they live!

> Children learn what they live!

Families are still the best vehicle for raising children. A loving, nurturing family unit of whatever form creates the kind of environment kids need to learn what's right and wrong and how to love themselves, too. Values are best included in an environment of love and acceptance.

Always take time to sit and talk to your kids. Don't be afraid to say what you feel, but don't ever be too closed to listen to what your kids think.

Always strive to teach your kids to love and respect themselves as children of God. A healthy love and respect for themselves is incredibly important for any kid. It's also the first step in helping a kid also learn a love and respect for those around him and God.

Parents – teenagers need you more than you think!

Honest Mistakes:
Have you ever wakened your spouse up early and said it was time to get up, you are late, but they didn't want to get up? Then you realize, after looking at the clock, that you make a mistake – it was 1:00 am not 7:00 am!

Grandparents – you really thought I was not going to include you in the parenting process? Being a good grandparent, beyond the love and affection you can give, grandchildren need you to be a friend and supporter, they need you to pray for them and provide spiritual guidance. In any relationship between grandparents and grandchildren their parents are still the key to the relationship grand-parents have with their grandchildren. If the grandparent does not have a good relationship with their son or daughter or son-in-law or daughter-in-law, it will be difficult to have a healthy, spiritual rela-tionship with their grandchildren. For many families this is not an issue, but if you have a less than perfect relationship with them, here's how prayer and understanding can help.

There are a couple things you can do to help the relationship:

First, *learn to listen* – you may want to tell your children how to raise your grandchildren, but more than anything you need to learn to listen to them as new parents and allow them to grow as a parent without you offering opinions. Grandparents, you are the sup-port system for your children, so you need to be kind and compas-sionate at all times. Next, grandparents you need to really fight the urge to disagree with your children on how they are raising your grandchildren. There will come a time when you don't agree with how your grandchildren are being raised, believe it. It might involve the way the parents discipline or don't discipline your grandchildren or it might be their change in religious preferences or no religious preference. While it might be difficult, try not to criticize the par-ents, especially in front of the grandchildren.

As grandparents we need to set the example and never worry if your grandchildren or your children are learning something or see-ing what we are doing. At some point in their life, they will remem-ber the things you said and the faith you had in God.

Instead of criticizing your children, set a prayerful example for them. Because of the inherent bond between grandparents and grandchildren, some children learn more of their spiritual and moral perspective from their grandparents than from any other role mod-els. In fact, this is a role many grandparents are eager to take on – to be the role models and set the example. If you ask any grandparent, they would list passing on morals and religion to their grandchildren as one of their top priorities. Grandparents teach more to their grand-children by experience and example than by preaching what they should do. Grandparents have unconditional love for their grand-children and grandchildren absorb more when there is no pressure.

If you are concerned about their religious upbringing, you might want to do the following two things. First, let them watch you. When your grandchildren spend time with you, be open about how you include God in your life. Just by the way you live your life you give them a moral and spiritual way to live.

The other thing you might want to do is read to your grandchildren or better yet have your grandchildren read bible stories or religious bedtime stories to you. The one thing we do with our grandchildren on Christmas Eve is to read Luke: 1 (Birth of Jesus) in the bible. We read the reason for Jesus' birth. But you need to explain the reason for the season and "Why" we are celebrating Christmas – the birth of Jesus. If your grandchildren live far away, you can call them and read or pray with them.

Sometimes, we grandparents forget our grandchildren are a little boy or girl. Let them be a little boy or girl. Laugh when they laugh. Cry when they cry. Suffer when they suffer. Bite your tongue when impatient words come. When you see them sleeping at nighttime it will hit you hard that they are still babies. Consider each day an opportunity to grow closer to your grandchildren.

How to Destroy Your Child
- Tell your child to do something 2 or 3 times so he will know that it is not important to follow direction on the first request.
- When your child misbehaves, yell and scream in an angry manner. This will "reward" your child's behavior. He is likely to get pleasure out of seeing that he can control and manipulate your emotions and that *you* will suffer for *their* misbehavior.
- Do things for your child that they are capable of doing for themselves.
- Call on your spouse to be the disciplinarian when the child misbehaves rather than handle it yourself.
- Allow your child to see that they can make you feel guilty by what they say.
- Give your children money or buy things when they ask for it instead or using an organized allowance system.
- Argue with your child.

- Get involved in fights between brothers and sisters. Question as to who started, play District Attorney. Take sides.

Memo from a Child
To: Parents

Don't spoil me. I know quite well that I ought not to have all I ask for – I'm only testing you.

Don't be afraid to be firm with me. I prefer it, it makes me feel secure.

Don't let me form bad habits. I have to rely on you to detect them in the early stages.

Don't make me feel smaller that I am. It only makes me behave stupidly "big."

Don't correct me in front of people if you can help it. I'll take much more notice if you talk quietly with me in private.

Don't make me feel that my mistakes are sins. It upsets my sense of values.

Don't protect me from consequences. I need to learn the painful way sometimes.

Don't be too upset when I say "I hate you." Sometimes it isn't you I hate but your power to thwart me.

Don't take too much notice of my small ailments. Sometimes they get me the attention I need.

Don't nag. If you do, I shall have to protect myself by appearing deaf.

Don't forget that I cannot explain myself as well as I should like. That is why I am not always accurate.

Don't put me off when I ask questions. If you do, you will find that I stop asking and seek my information elsewhere.

Don't be inconsistent. That completely confuses me and makes me lose faith in you.

Don't tell me my fears are silly. They are terribly real, and you can do much to reassure me if you try to understand.

Don't ever suggest that you are perfect or infallible. It gives me too great a shock when I discover that you are neither.

Don't ever think that it is beneath your dignity to apologize to me. An honest apology makes me feel surprisingly warm towards you.

Don't forget I love experimenting. I couldn't get along without it, so please put up with it.

Don't forget how quickly I am growing up. It must be very difficult for you to keep pace with me, but please do try.

Don't forget that I don't thrive without lots of love and understanding, but I don't need to tell you, do I?

Please keep yourself fit and healthy. I need you.

(Source Unknown)

Things My MOTHER Taught Me

My Mother taught me LOGIC …
*"If you fall off that swing and break your neck,
you can't go to the store with me."*

My Mother taught me MEDICINE …
*"If you don't stop crossing your eyes,
they're going to freeze that way."*

My Mother taught me TO THINK AHEAD …
*"If you don't pass your spelling test,
you'll never get a good job."*

My Mother taught me ESP …
*"Put your sweater on; don't you think I know
when you're cold?"*

My Mother taught me HUMOR …
*"When that lawn mower cuts off your toes,
don't come running to me."*

My Mother taught me how to BECOME AN ADULT …
"If you don't eat your vegetables, you'll never grow up."

My Mother taught me GENETICS …
"You are just like your father!"

My Mother taught me about my ROOTS …
"Do you think you were born in a barn?"

My Mother taught me about the WISDOM OF AGE …
"When you get to be my age, you will understand."

My Mother taught me about ANTICIPATION …
"Just wait until your father gets home."

My Mother taught me about RECEIVING …
"You are going to get it when we get home."

My mom taught me about LOVE …
I am here for you and I will give you all that I have."
And she thought no one was listening.

(Excerpt from St. Peter Catholic Church bulletin May 12, 2013)

Now take 5 minutes and read Proverbs 22.

Don't read another chapter until you write one thing you have learned from your readings today that will help you become a better person.

_____

_____

_____

_____

_____

_____

_____

_____

_____

_____
_____
_____
_____
_____
_____
_____
_____
_____
_____
_____
_____
_____
_____
_____
_____
_____
_____
_____
_____
_____
_____
_____

Proverbs 22:6 - Train up a child in the way he should go,
even when he is old, he will not depart from it.

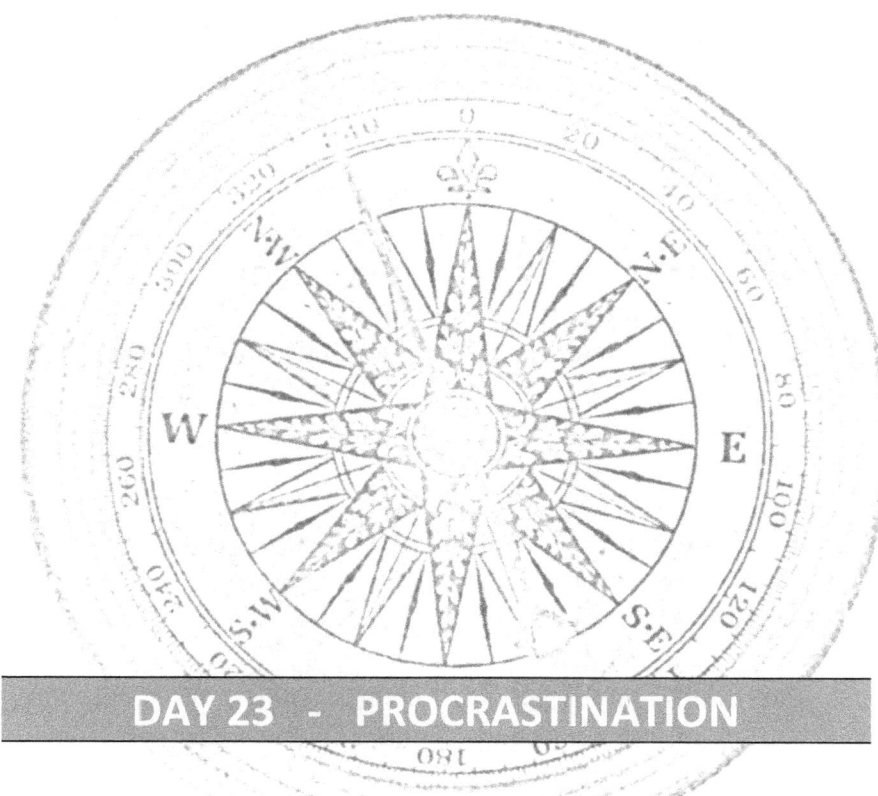

DAY 23 - PROCRASTINATION

*2 Thessalonians 3:10-12 - Anyone unwilling to work should
not eat. For we hear that some of you are living in idleness,
mere busy bodies not doing any work. Now such persons we
command and exhort in the Lord Jesus Christ to do their
work quietly and to earn their own living.*

How often do we spend time and effort trying to figure out the
best methods, the proper techniques, the perfect words until you lose
the momentum to actually do anything? How often do we lose the
potential blessings that God puts in our paths? I remember a story
of a little turtle dove chick left stranded on a step at school and the
mother turtle dove waited for the turtle dove chick to get down from
the step by itself. You agonize over whether you should help, but
you were always told that if you handle a baby bird, the mother will
abandon the chick since it had a human smell. You ponder how you

can get the chick down from the step without touching it. You thought maybe you could get a shoe box and scoop the chick up off the step and put the chick close to the mother bird. You go inside to find a box. You look out the window to see some facility mainte- nance worker picking up the chick off the step with gloves on. The point is that at some point you have to make a decision.

The most important moment in your life is right now. Don't let hesitation and procrastination keep you from your destiny. Procrastination is the symp- tom; fear is the problem. Putting off a simple thing makes it hard and putting off a hard thing makes it impossible.

> The most important moment in our life is right now!

Why don't we jump at opportunities as quickly as we jump to conclusions? Procrastination is the grave in which opportunity is buried. Anybody who brags about what he is going to do tomorrow, will probably do the same thing he did yesterday.

Two things that rob people of their peace of mind: work unfin- ished and work not yet begun. Tackle any challenge at first sight: the longer you stare at it, the bigger it becomes, the lazier a man is, the more he is going to do tomorrow.

When you have no more time available to do your work – that's when you start procrastinating. That no more time in most cases is self-inflicted.

Do you procrastinate at work? I know sometimes at work if I am not sure what to do with a particular document or action, I put it to the side and come back to it later. If you handle that piece of paper more than once, you are procrastinating.

The unhappiest people are those who can never make a deci- sion. An indecisive person can never be said to belong to them- selves. Don't worry about not making a decision; if you wait long enough someone else will make it for you. You can't grow while letting others make decisions for you. Indecisive people are like a blind man looking in a dark room for a black cat that isn't there. No decision is a decision. Remain indecisive and you will never grow.

To the vacillating and floundering mind, everything is impossible because it seems so. Don't wait for extraordinary circumstances to do good; make use of ordinary situations.

Have you ever noticed how well a person maintains their car, as far as washing the outside or keeping the inside of their car clean? This reflects their ability to be organized. Over the years in management, I have noticed a few things about a person and whether they are organized or a procrastinator. I can honestly say that when I see how a person maintains their car that 99% of the time, I can tell you if they are an organized person or if they procrastinate. You might be saying this is hard to believe, but when you look inside their car and it is dirty and not neat, it also means that they will probably not keep their workspace neat and clean either and are very disorganized and they procrastinate.

You are saying to yourself that this is hard to believe, try it for yourself and you will see for yourself.

Here is the thing about new inventions. They all begin as ideas, but they become reality only when someone says yes and begins working on them. Through trial and error, dedication and faith Johannes Gutenberg invented the printing press, Alexander Graham Bell invented the telephone and Lawrence Roberts developed the Internet. Just think if they would have procrastinated for decades. Procrastination can be overcome, and you definitely can learn to make decisions timely.

Now take 5 minutes and read Proverbs 23.

Don't read another chapter until you write one thing you have learned from your readings today that will help you become a better person.

_____

_____

_____

_____

_____

_____

Proverbs 23:12 - Apply your heart to instruction
and your ears to words of knowledge.

DAY 24 - MOTIVATION

2 Corinthians 12:9 - My grace is sufficient for you, for my power is made perfect in weakness.

Every weakness you have is an opportunity for God to show His strength in your life.

Motivation: I enjoyed playing football growing up and wanted to be my best. As I was growing up there was a coach named Vince Lombardi, the famed Green Bay Packers football coach who was a feared disciplinarian. But he was also a great motivator. One day he chewed out a player who had missed several blocking assignments. After practice Lombardi stormed into the locker room and saw that the player was sitting at his locker, head down, dejected. Lombardi mussed his hair, patted him on the shoulders, and said, "one of these days you're going to be the best guard in the NFL. That player was Jerry Kramer, and Kramer says he carried that positive image of himself for the rest of his career. "Lombardi's encouragement had a tremendous impact on my whole life," Kramer said. He went on to become a member of the Green Bay Packers Hall of Fame and a member of the NFL's All 50-Year-Team.

Everybody needs motivation from time to time. A kind word said in a positive way does wonders for your motivation. Motivation makes it possible to accomplish what you should accomplish. Never underestimate the power of motivation. Motivation helps people change their lives by developing a better commitment, habit, or path for success.

Our desire to excel helps us exceed our expectations!

Self-motivators learn how to "pat themselves on their backs" and still be humble. For most of us, there are times when we feel underappreciated, as if no one understands how hard we are working and how much we are trying.

Strength does not come from winning. Your struggles develop your strengths. When you go through hardships and decide not to surrender that is strength. I got more motivated when I was told that I couldn't do something, especially when I felt I really could.

How to Stay Motivated:
- ✓ Take it one day at a time
- ✓ Surround yourself with positivity
- ✓ Create a vision board
- ✓ Make smart goals (see Day 28)
- ✓ Reward yourself
- ✓ Believe in yourself
- ✓ Recognize your progress
- ✓ Visualize accomplishing your goals
- ✓ Be kind to yourself
- ✓ Don't compare yourself to others

Enthusiasm always makes others stand up and take notice. Nothing significant was ever achieved without enthusiasm.

Self-disciplined people have been able to beat the disease of procrastination. The self-disciplined person is the individual whose feet hit the floor the moment the alarm rings in the morning – actually they wake up 5 minutes before the alarm goes off! Either way, they do not push the snooze button. I remember when I first got married to my current wife, Michele. When the alarm went off, I got out of bed and started doing the things I needed to do. My wife thought something was wrong and I said no, it was time to get up. She always set the clock 10 minutes ahead and laid back down for a few minutes before getting up. If you are looking for leaders, you should select those people who have a high sense of self-discipline – you can really count on those people. The people who are discipline seem to work and get things done better then the people who aren't self-disciplined.

One of my favorite pieces of advice has always been to praise often and tell people how much you appreciate them. One way I did this is at work was by developing the "Pat on the Back" award for Hernando County. I thought it was very important to immediately recognize employees for something good they had demonstrated such as:

- Customer Service
- Integrity
- Teamwork
- Leadership
- Positive Attitude
- Creativity
- Superior Performance

Tell people how much you appreciate them.

Sometimes we can get going in overdrive and forget to pause and reflect on what we have done or accomplished. When we take a moment to reflect, we can regain our perspective and realize that we are making a valuable contribution to families, co-workers, humanity and ourselves. Recognizing your contribution from within yourself is actually more powerful and satisfying than hearing it from someone else. In fact, if you are self-disciplined and a type "A" personality you will identify with this. To feel good about yourself and your efforts you must be able to recognize and acknowledge your contribution and efforts. Almost everyone loves to be patted on the back by others. Even if you don't want to admit it – it feels good!

80/20 Rule:

You probably have heard about the 80/20 rule at some point in your life. If not, this is what it is – allegedly in the workplace, 20 percent of the people do approximately 80 percent of the work. Is this motivation or simply the rule? I think that most people don't work hard enough and almost no one lives up to their full potential. A lot of time when a person is not motivated or as productive as they could be, they are too busy worrying about what other people are doing at work or worrying about their family situation. They need to put more emphasis on what they can get out of their own level of productivity. The over-achievers have a hard time understanding that other people have different priorities, work ethics, comfort levels, abilities, and mindsets. The other key factor is that different people also define productivity in very different ways.

> ### *It's not about how bad you want it!*
> ### *It's about how hard*
> ### *You're willing to work for it!*

Now take 5 minutes and read Proverbs 24.

Don't read another chapter until you write one thing you have learned from your readings today that will help you become a better person.

_____

_____

_____

_____

_____

Proverbs 24:3 - By Wisdom is a house built,
by understanding is it made firm.

DAY 25 - FITNESS/WELLNESS

1 Corinthians 9:26-27 - So, therefore, I run, not with uncertainty. So I fight, not as one who beats the air. But I bring and keep my body under subjection, lest when preaching to others I myself should be disqualified.

Today is my tomorrow.
It's up to me to shape it,
To take control
And seize every opportunity.

The power is in the choices
I make each day.
I eat well, I live well.
I shape me.

(unknown)

Improving your health improves your quality of life. Before you start any fitness program, make sure you see your doctor and get a medical checkup. Fitness is not about being better than someone else – it's about being better than you used to be!

Why is fitness important to you? Here are a few reasons it should be important to you. Believe it or not, being fit makes you feel better and gives you more energy. Fitness is **Leave all of your excuses behind and look ahead.** only one part of your wellness. The other part is making healthy food choices. Everybody's body makeup is different, but we all must eat to live, and we must eat right. How? When you start reading this chapter please remember one thing, you must commit, commit, and commit to the fitness program, you are willing to stick to doing. Before you start doing any fitness or workout program, you must always stretch out/warm up and you stretch out and cool down when finishing your fitness program. Always check with your doctor or your personal fitness trainer before you start a fitness program.

Increase your water intake and decrease refined sugar from your meals. Many times, I have been told the formula for maintaining a healthy weight is to eat a balanced diet and exercise regularly. Everybody knows the formula, although sophisticated marketers' package it in many creative ways. If we all know what the formula is, why is it so difficult to apply it to our lives? The secret to losing weight is not knowing the formula – it is applying what we already know. Most important of all:

You Must Believe in Yourself!

Fitness is often the first thing we put aside as we hurry through our fast-paced lives. Our hectic lifestyle and travel schedules have most of us eating on the go and at fast food restaurants. We sacrifice eating healthy for eating quickly because of our fast-paced world and technology devices.

Our fitness is critical to our overall satisfaction both physical and emotional. Believe it or not, you feel better when you exercise and feel good about your body. I remember when I was in the Air Force, I ran every day at lunchtime. I had more energy and felt good all day. It seemed like I had two days in one. I had day one in the morning and day two in the afternoon. In other words, I felt like I had two mornings in a day. I had as much energy in the afternoon as I had first thing in the morning. I relaxed when I ran, and my mind was free to think. I think I solved my problems or situations more while I ran versus sitting at my desk. My staff finally realized what was going on and they used to wait until I came back from running. They would ask, "So what did you solve today?"

If you decide to run, a key factor is to drink water before you run and right after you finish. I ran in all kinds of weather and I always reminded myself to drink the water before and after.
Family Fitness – Fast Fun: I remember when I was stationed in Germany how on Sundays the German nationals would walk with their families on all the trails through the forest. They were staying fit, doing it as a family and having fun!

Book: "Walk Yourself Thin!" by David A. Rives

One important thing that the author of "Walk Yourself Thin!" points out which I think is very interesting is "you can forget about losing weight with thin walking." What? That's right – thin walking isn't your typical weight lost program or what you would call a diet. It's an exercise program and exercise programs work differently than diets. With thin walking, two things happen: a pound of fat still disappears, but now a pound of new muscle shows up in its place. So, at the end of each thin walking day, instead of being "one pound short" like you were on your diet, you find that you're "no pounds short," but you're still one pound skinnier. Wait a minute – how can that be? How can I be skinnier without losing any weight? Easy because a pound of muscle takes up a lot less space that a pound of fat.

Fitness at Work: Yes, you can do a few things at work and feel good about yourself. First, you can walk up and down the stairs instead of taking the elevator. If you don't have any stairs at work, then you can walk at lunch time or during your breaks. You can also do a few exercises while sitting at your desk which will make you feel better, especially if you do a lot of work on the computer. The more you are able to exercise, the better you will feel.

Post work out recovery meals should replace lost electrolytes, sodium, and carbohydrates (good carbs). Your body needs the proper fuel to maintain maximum performance.

Everyone goes through their own personal battles with fitness and eating right. Some of you will need some encouragement from a personal trainer and others are self-disciplined enough and can do their workouts and fitness training and healthy eating on their own. Each of us has dreamed of doing a few things before we get too old to enjoy them. What is on your bucket list? Our desire to excel helps us exceed our expectations.

Leave all your excuses behind and look ahead to being fit and healthy. You can do it!

Now take 5 minutes and read Proverbs 25.

Don't read another chapter until you write one thing you have learned from your readings today that will help you become a better person.

_____

_____

_____

_____

_____

_____

_____

_____

_____

_____

_____

_____

_____
_____
_____
_____
_____
_____
_____
_____
_____
_____
_____
_____
_____
_____
_____
_____
_____
_____
_____
_____
_____
_____
_____
_____
_____
_____
_____
_____
_____
_____

Proverbs 25:16 - If you find honey, eat only what you need,
lest you become glutted with it and vomit it up.

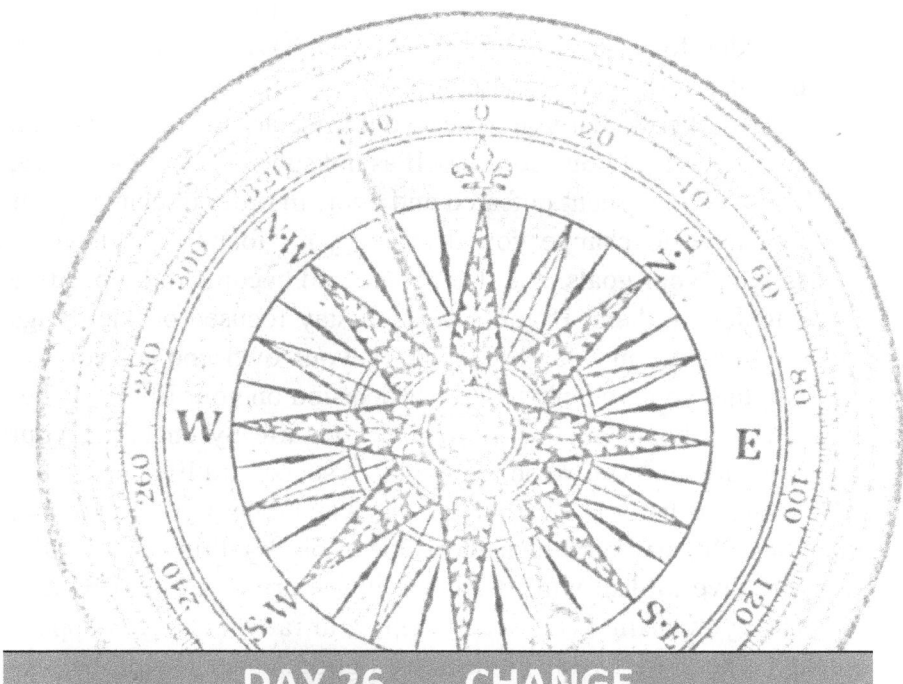

DAY 26 - CHANGE

Psalm 120:1 - I took my troubles to the Lord;
I cried out to him, and he answered my prayer.
Proverbs 23:7 As a man thinketh in his heart, so is he.
Change is not easy!
Change requires action!

For example: many people do not eat broccoli cooked or raw, but you can change the taste of it by putting butter, salt and pepper and cooking it or by dipping the raw broccoli in Ranch dressing, surprising most people will eat the broccoli.

Life, like a trip to the moon, is full of changes and adjustments. Nothing is as permanent as change.

Everyone wants to change the world, but no one thinks of changing themselves.

When people think they can't change, they stop growing. Life changes when our habits change.

In order for your life to change you have to change. Your dreams only work if you put in the work.

Did you know that you never would rise above the image you have of yourself? If you see yourself as not successful and a failure, then your life may seem defeated and poor. In order to change your life, you have to change your life and your focus. You have to change what your goals, and dreams are and become more positive about achieving them. If you choose to stay focused on the things that are negative in your life, then by your own choice, you are agreeing that you are defeated. Your decision on your life is the deciding vote. If you choose to change your life by changing your goals and dreams, you're on the road to a successful life.

Change is hard. But driving change can be harder if you do not have the right person as the leader. One of biggest things as a leader that you have to deal with is change in the organization. I believe that when you change your leadership, your rate of change happens quickly. There are two (2) questions a good leader should be prepared to address quickly:

What if?

Why not?

When you are in management, you must be a leader who is willing to look at the organization with open eyes.

Why are we doing this? Why are we *not* doing this? Sometimes there are legitimate reasons that certain changes and process improvements cannot or have not been implemented. However, ask yourself the question- What if – can you improve the organization and what if the process is more efficient and effective.

I have been doing construction contracts for over twenty years. Change orders are common for construction contracts no matter if they are contracts issued by a government agency or the private sector. The most common forms of change I see deal with the changes in the original plans, design problems, unforeseen site

> When people think they can't change, they stop growing.

conditions, or material shortages. If I asked you to tell me the three R's, many of you would tell me "Reading, writing and arithmetic." But the Three R's I'm referring to are: "Responsive, Receptive, and Reasonable."

"Responsive" means acting appropriately regarding the issues at hand, rather than being driven and controlled by knee jerk reactions and quick actions. Responsive means having the ability to see the whole picture and the perspective to look at alternative ways to do things. A responsive person can look at all the variables and facts and make a decision to change direction.

"Receptive" implies being open to ideas and suggestions. People who are receptive are willing to look at all sides of the situation. A receptive person encourages input from others and is not defensive if someone recommends a new way to do something.

"Reasonable" suggests the ability to see things fairly without self-serving justification. Being reasonable includes the ability to put yourself in the shoes of others, being able to see the bigger picture, and to maintain perspective. Reasonable people are able to see beyond their own desires and needs, which makes them compassionate and helpful to others.

If you can strive to be responsive, receptive, and reasonable, my guess is that, most everything else will fall into place and take care of itself. If you want to change what is going on around you, you must change what is going on inside you.

Change is a perplexing thing – especially personal change. We all know how hard it is and sometimes I wonder "why" it takes a major personal catastrophe (and then sometimes even that doesn't work) for any of us to institute new steps in our lives.

I keep thinking that there are things I'd like to change, but yet, do I really have to wait until I am diagnosed with heart disease, cancer, something serious, or perhaps a loss of someone important in my life in order to muster the energy and resolve to make the desired changes?

Nothing is as permanent as change.

Yes, I am also aware that sometimes in the midst of the challenges and both the need and desire for change, a gentle word is not sufficient, that indeed it takes more – much more. Something along the lines of a "strong driving wind" or encouragement for you to make up your mind is necessary. On occasion, it proves to be true that some of the larger than life train wrecks in our lives are actually the result of our having missed or refused to act upon a series of opportunities for change.

We all keep thinking that we'd like to change, but guess what we procrastinate or think we can do it later? There are some things you don't want to wait until it is too late, like taking care of your health. You need to take care of yourself and get your checkups regularly. I remember I had an annual checkup because my insurance company paid me $50.00 to get an annual physical. Well, during my annual physical in 1998, I had a mole on my left arm in the triceps area that was starting to get bigger and discolored. My doctor said he was going to refer me to a dermatologist to look at it. I said sure, but I put it off for a couple of months and when I finally went in, it was not good news. After they did a couple of biopsies it turned out to be stage 3 melanoma skin cancer. The doctor wanted to do surgery immediately and within a week I had the surgery and I am thankful and blessed that all has been well.

We shake our heads and say things like "if only I had known" or "if only I had listened to my heart" the first and second time I felt this way. We are not always the best judges of which approach is the best.

I'm finally "getting it" after much heartbreaking disappointment and self-imposed pressure. I need to expect the unexpected, to be flexible, to roll with the punches then no matter what transpires, I'll be ready and those around me will be relieved. Often those Plan A and Plan B times turn out to be more fun, more memorable, and more rewarding than what had originally been planned anyway.

"Anyone can make short-term temporary changes; champions pursue permanent change and never ever give up." (Unknown on Poster)

Now take 5 minutes and read Proverbs 26.

Don't read another chapter until you write one thing you have
learned from your readings today that will help you become a
better person.

_____
_____
_____
_____
_____
_____
_____
_____
_____
_____
_____
_____
_____
_____
_____
_____
_____
_____
_____
_____
_____
_____
_____
_____
_____
_____
_____
_____
_____
_____

Proverbs 26:12 - You see a man wise in his own eyes? There is more hope for a fool than for him.

DAY 27 - SUCCESS

Luke 18:27 - And he said, what is impossible
for human beings is possible for God.

"When you want to succeed as badly as you want to breathe, then
you will be successful." Eric Thomas

Success: No one is going to hand you success – you must go out
and get it yourself. That's why I'm here. To dominate, to conquer -
both the world and myself.

The only place that success comes before work
is in the dictionary.
If you have the courage to begin,
you have the courage to succeed.
There will always be someone more talented than you.

Remember you are not running the race,
but your race will be how you run.

How do you see people in the world around you and what assumptions do you tend to make about them? Too many times we are not thankful. God puts us at the right place at the right time and sometimes we do not even realize it.

Share your smile with someone – they might need it today.

Why people are not successful in life is because they make excuses, have roadblocks, distractions, and illusions that are keeping them from experiencing success, joy, peace, prosperity, and achievement in life.

Excuses are like clouds in the sky! We all make excuses! An excuse is a universally accepted lie about why we don't do something we want or ought to do.

Reasons do exist however, but not many. The difference between an excuse and a reason is that in the end an excuse is *our choice*.

We all can come up with many excuses but here are some common ones:

NO TIME, TOO OLD, TOO YOUNG, TOO LAZY, NO MONEY, TOO SHY, I CAN'T TALK, NOT EDUCATED, FEAR, LIES, TOO TIRED, MY DOG NEEDS ME, MY FAMILY NEEDS ME, MY FRIENDS NEED ME ...

You need to change your STINKING THINKING and tell yourself this: I refuse to lose, I refuse to have excuses, I refuse to be negative, I refuse to whine, I refuse to accept failure, I refuse to accept defeat, I refuse to settle for less and I refuse to give up.

You never know where success might take you. So, always dress for success. Don't look at being perfect but look at doing your best all the time. Success is measured by your terms. I remember growing up in a family of 5 boys and being told and overhearing people talking and saying those Wetherington boys are good boys, but they will never amount to anything. Boy, were all those people wrong! Thanks to our mother - Annabelle Kersey Wetherington; she taught us the value of hard work and honesty.

Here is what the five of us amounted to:

Jack Wetherington – Served in the Navy, Bachelors and Masters (MBA) Degree from University of North Florida with emphasis in Accounting, and successful Civil Service career as an Auditor and Financial Manager for the Navy and retired from the Civil Service.

Clifford Wetherington – He was the first of us to attend college; successful in retail services.

Russell Wetherington – Graduate of the University of Nebraska at Omaha with a Bachelor General Studies degree; graduate of the Air Force ROTC Program (Distinguished Graduate) and commissioned officer in the USAF; retired Major Air Force; served as President of Florida Association Public Procurement Officer Association and currently the Assistant County Administrator at Hernando County, Florida.

George Wetherington – Career in law Enforcement, Retired Deputy Sheriff, St. Johns County, Florida.

Wayne Wetherington – Veteran USAF, Business Manager, Technical Support to over 6,500 Northeast Realtors and provides training courses for the realtors. Studied Computer Information Systems at Florida Community College, Jacksonville.

The central challenge for unsuccessful people is not having a plan. Face the challenge instead of running away from it. If you want that new job, how do you get it or get qualified for the job? You need to develop a plan. Your plan needs to look at education, experience, and training requirements first. Then you need to look at how you interview; you may need to interview better. How do you learn to interview better? You need to take a class or go to someone who knows how to interview and learn what you can do better. Some suggestions to interview better, start with reading books on interviewing and Google the Internet for interviewing techniques. Look at interview questions for the type of job you want. Be prepared! Dress neatly, clean, sharp.

You don't need to be perfect; just do your best *all* the time.

One warning about the education excuse – many people put off doing what they ought to because they have taken some night or on-line courses and they thought it took a lot of their time. At some point you need to make a decision to get your college degree. I can attest to that because I was taking night courses for a few years and I finally felt like I was not getting anywhere. I had been in the Air Force for about six years and was working at a military hospital as an Optometry Technician and realized I could go to college and get a degree like some of the other people I worked with. I made a decision and applied for an educational discharge to enroll in the Air Force ROTC training program at the University of Nebraska at Omaha (UNO) and was accepted. The only problem was that I had to complete 3 years of college courses in a 2-year period because the ROTC program was only a 2-year program. That meant that I had to take day and night classes at the same time and also take summer classes. I would be lying to you if I told you it was easy, it was not. But, if I can do it, you sure can do it, too. You see, I was not the most academic student in high school. I was lucky to "C" myself through high school, but I did very good in college.

Do you have good or bad habits? When you look at successful people, you look at their habits. If you really look deep down at their Rock-solid habits, you will see that these habits are things they do all the time and these habits have made them great.

If you really look at your habits, you need to honestly decide which habits are bad and decide to get rid of those bad habits. You need to focus on your good habits and work on forgetting those bad habits. Don't get me wrong it's hard to get rid of those bad habits and there may be some that you truly don't want to get rid of. However, you must develop those good habits that are going to knock those bad habits out of your life for good. It may take developing many little good habits to knock out that one BIG BAD habit, but you can do it.

If you struggle with getting rid of that annoying BAD habit, remember that your life will always have many mountains and valleys you will have to deal with and with time you will be on the Top of the mountain and you will be able to get rid of that BAD habit.

Play to Win!

Excerpt from Ricki Taylor's Motivational Moment, 1/31/14

Success and failure are actually closely aligned to the point that success is not possible without failure. Most people live their lives trying to avoid failure and the pain and depression that can go with falling short of a goal or task.

The reality is success, in whatever form it might be, comes from how we "play the game." Often if you are watching the sport of football, a team will go up by several touchdowns and suddenly decide to be conservative. The winning team does not want to make mistakes so they begin to run the ball every down which ends up in three downs and a punt. On defense they go into a prevent mode in order to avoid the easy score from a long touchdown.

The losing team suddenly begins to gain more momentum because they get the ball more often and are able to move the ball downfield quickly because the defense is willing to give up short to medium passes because they are trying to stop the "big play." What happens? The losing team catches up and in many cases ends up winning!

It seems that most people spend their lives "playing not to lose" versus "playing to win." Playing not to lose involves the following:

Not taking chances due to fear of failure.

Avoiding any form of risk.

Having a mentality that losing is a possibility.

Believing that others are more worthy of success.

Thinking that luck is never on their side.

Feeling undeserving of true success.

> *Taking inconsistent action.*
>
> *Playing to win is a totally different mentality:*
> *Calculated risk is a part of the winning mentality.*
> *A belief that winners deserve success.*
> *Taking action on a consistent basis.*
> *Having mental discipline to stay on task.*
> *Being excited about pushing beyond any comfort zone.*

American President Theodore Roosevelt said the following:

"Far better is it to dare things, to win glorious triumphs, even though checkered by failure... than to rank with those poor spirits who neither enjoy nor suffer much, because they live in a gray twilight that knows not victory nor defeat."

Get in the game! Life is meant to be lived to the fullest. Your destiny, your life is totally in your hands. Charge forward and let every failure take you one step closer to triumph!

So, don't let anyone tell you that you can't do something.

Three Steps to Success

- **Decide** what you want
- **Determine** the Plan and the Price you will have to pay to achieve it
- **Commit** to pay the Price

Deciding what you want is your starting point. Decision time!

Determine the Plan-This is called setting goals and will be covered in the next chapter.

Commit by working to achieve those goals.

> *You can run after satisfaction,*
> *but satisfaction must come from within!*

Now take 5 minutes and read Proverbs 27.

Don't read another chapter until you write one thing you have learned from your readings today that will help you become a better person.

_____

_____

_____

_____

_____

_____

_____

_____

_____

_____

_____

_____

_____

_____

_____

_____

_____

_____

_____

_____

_____

_____

_____

_____

_____

_____

_____

_____

_____

Proverbs 27:2 - Let another praise you, not your own mouth; someone else, not your own lips.

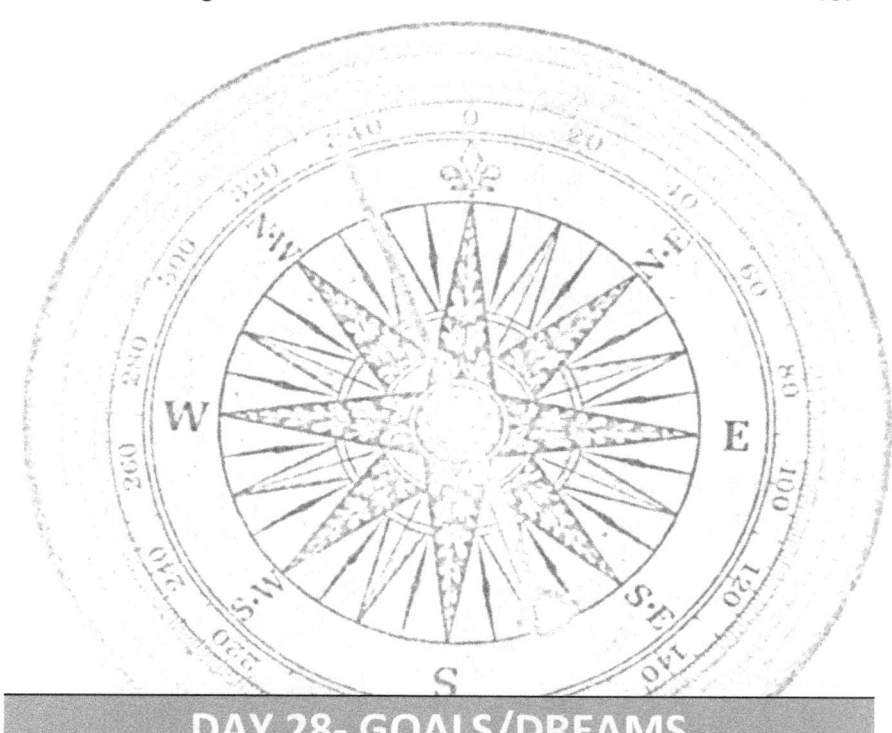

DAY 28- GOALS/DREAMS

Ecclesiastes 5:3 - A dream comes through much activity.

Too often people want to tear you down, you are not educated, you are not smart enough, or you are from the wrong family. Just because someone does not believe in you, remember it is in you; if you have a Dream, believe in yourself. People don't determine your destiny, you do! Who told you couldn't do something? Take control of your image, your life and your dream. You need people around you, who are positive and who are there to build you up.

It is often said that the toughest step to take when starting an overwhelming task is the first step, but I don't think that's true.

Once you decide to accomplish a difficult task, it's the second step that is the toughest and the one that really counts. Once a decision is made to start, that is in essence the first step. It requires no effort, just decision. It is acting on that decision (the second step) that truly begins to lead toward your goal.

I love the phrase "baby steps." When you are prepared to accomplish any task, whether a part of your job or a lifetime dream, it is easy to get discouraged when you look down the road and see overwhelming obstacles. In fact, most people throw in the towel at this point. I call this the "separation point." It might be the single biggest reason the world is filled with "dreamers" versus "doers."

There are many ways to develop and start goal setting. I have read many books and attended seminars on goal setting and goals. However, one thing I have learned is that you must keep it simple. Take a blank sheet of paper and write down on the paper everything you want to do, achieve, or own. Set your time for 15 minutes to do this. Now take your list and put a 1, 3, 5, 7, or 10 by each one to represent in how many years you want to achieve the goal.

I recommend you use Ken Blanchard's SMART Goal Format from the "One Minute Manger" books in order for your goal to be accomplished in year one. SMART Goals answer these questions:

Specific
- What exactly is the goal or task?
- When does the goal or task need to be accomplished?

Motivating
- Is the goal or task meaningful to the individual?
- Will working on this goal build competence or commitment?
- Will working on this goal add or drain ENERGY?

Attainable
- Is the goal realistic, reasonable, and achievable?
- Is the goal within the individual's control?

Relevant
- Is the goal or task meaningful work for the organization?
- Is the goal or task aligned with organization and work team goals?
- Is the goal or task high priority in relation to other goals?

Trackable

- What does a good job look like at each level of development?
- How will progress and results be measured and tracked?

Smart goals motivate.

Remember that you are using the SWAG rule to determine how long you think it will take to achieve the goals. You ask what does SWAG stand for? It stands for Scientific Wild Ass Guess (SWAG). Remember this is only a guess or a target for you to shoot for to achieve your goals.

When Setting Goals

- Choose goals in areas you have control over
- Always use positive terms in goal setting
- Be brief
- Make it emotional
- Believe
- Take immediate action
- Last year was practice
- This year is warm up
- Next year is game time

If you truly want to accomplish a dream, task, or goal, here is a simple "baby step," guide to success:

- ✓ Break down your ultimate dream or goal into the smallest steps possible.
- ✓ Take one action each day toward the dream or goal.
- ✓ Reward yourself for even the smallest action!
- ✓ Have a mentor or accountability partner to remind you of your goal or dream.

Never stop taking those second, third, and fourth steps! Too simple? Every great accomplishment in the entire history of mankind has followed these steps. We often assume that only talented people accomplish great things. That's not true. Persistent people accomplish great things! Are you ready? Decide to get started and then take that second step!

A goal is a dream with a deadline! Dreams are goals written down. Dare to dream!

Proverbs 16:3 - Commit your work to the Lord and your plans will be established.

It is amazing how events can inspire us and not just in our childhood dreams.

It starts when we're young. We dream about being a fireman, policeman or ballerina and then just like that we reach that point where we can't wait until that magical age called "teenagers." But 13 is a whole lot like 12, so we start looking forward to the freedom of age 16. The novelty of driving wears off quickly though and we start thinking about how great life will be when we graduate from high school and college. After that things like landing our ideal job, getting married, and having kids become our focus. It never stops. There is always something ahead that threatens to steal our focus even if it is just looking forward to the weekend. Left unchecked, those things have the power to prevent us from doing anything meaningful today. It's not bad to look forward to things, but life is short. It is not part of God's plan to waste any moment, day, week, or stage of your life. It is not His plan for you to focus on tomorrow because truthfully tomorrow is a mystery. You don't know what tomorrow will bring.

Don't let negative people and negative thoughts steal your dream!

Whether you're looking forward to something or dreading it, the lesson is the same: God never intends for the focus on tomorrow to be your focus today.

Do not let negative people and negative thoughts steal your dream! We all have dreams, but in order to make dreams come into reality it takes an awful lot of determination, dedication, self-discipline, and effort.

Choose goals based on your priorities. Be specific when you choose goals. Organize your life to accomplish those goals. Commit yourself wholeheartedly to those goals. Adjust your goals when it is obvious to do so. Choose a time each week to plan your schedule.

How do you orchestrate life so that you are on a consistent path of improvement?
- You will choose to listen to certain advice in your life
- You will make decisions based on this advice
- Your decisions will influence your emotions, which either add or drain energy from your pursuit
- Your energy level determines the effectiveness of your efforts
- Those who consistently grow in experience will achieve some level of success in every season of their life.

The person with imagination is never alone and never finished.

You were built for creativity. Your eyes look for opportunity, your ears listen for direction, your mind requires a challenge, and your heart longs for God's way. Your heart sees what the brain knows nothing of.

Make a daily demand on your creativity. Everything starts as somebody's daydream. All people of action are first dreamers. Many times, we act or fail to act not because of will as is so commonly believed, but because of imagination. Your dreams are an indicator of your potential greatness. Other people may be smarter, better educated, or more experienced than you, but no single person has a corner on dreams, desire, or ambition.

Don't downgrade your dreams to match your reality. Upgrade your faith to match your destiny.

Keep your vision in front of you no matter what your vision is: house, car, job, family, or baby. You always need to keep your vision in front of you – use pictures! A lot of people tell themselves, "Well, I can't even imagine that happening to me." Don't worry, it won't happen if you don't believe it will. If you don't have a vision for it, it's not going to happen. Without a vision, you won't see it happen. You won't be a winner if you don't believe.

The problem is you're being limited by your own imagination. You've got to change what you're seeing. Don't let negative thoughts paint you a wrong picture. Use your imagination to see yourself accomplishing those dreams, rising higher, overcoming obstacles, being healthy, strong, blessed, and prosperous.

Seeing is believing!

It's more valuable to look where you're going than to see where you've been. Don't see your future only from yesterday's perspective. Follow your passion/path – do not give up.

Settling
(Excerpt from Ricki Taylor's Motivational Moment)

There is a silent, slow destroyer of dreams. It quietly invades lives, enters the human brain and remains, sometimes for weeks, sometimes years, often a lifetime.

It is unrecognizable to most people as it silently robs us, like a pickpocket. Most people never even realize that anything is missing. The stealer of dreams, the roadblock to greatness, is "settling." It is taking what life gives us, never questioning that we could have had more or been more. Ask life for a penny and that is all you will receive. Ask it for more, and it will give up its riches.

Settling starts early in life and is present in everything from relationships to jobs. How many people are in relationships that are unfulfilling or jobs they do not like because they believe that is all they deserve? The numbers are staggering! A Gallop Poll estimated that over 60% of people are dissatisfied with their job. Settling does not necessarily mean staying in a job or relationship you do not like. More often, it is not taking full advantage of your present situation, not expanding your horizons.

Here is a powerful statement: "Settling is only a state of mind." It is a decision to accept less than what you deserve and through not taking action you reinforce that you are correct, your life is going nowhere. Part of the problem is people are afraid of making the wrong decision should they take a chance. There is no wrong decision when you decide to reach for more, to become all you want to be. The failures and wrong decisions become minor setbacks and in reality, guideposts to the right decisions and actions!

TAKE A MINUTE
Look at your goals
Look at your performance
See if your behavior matches your goals

Now take 5 minutes and read Proverbs 28.

Don't read another chapter until you write one thing you have learned from your readings today that will help you become a better person.

_____

_____

_____

_____

_____

_____

_____

_____

_____

_____

_____

_Proverbs 28:20 - The trustworthy man will be richly blessed,
he who is in haste to grow rich will not go unpunished._

DAY 29- PATIENCE

Philippians 4:6-7 - Do not be anxious about anything, but in every situation, by prayer and petition, with thanksgiving, present your request to God.

Patience is required throughout our lives. Seldom do things come out exactly as we would like them to be. Seldom do others act as we would like them to act. Life seems to be a series of "put-up-withs" rather than a place of enjoyment, of "likes." Sometimes we wait a long time before the answer to our situation or desire is truly answered.

Those in between days – days of waiting can be exciting if we are anticipating something enjoyable and happy; birthdays, gradua-tions, weddings, and the return of someone you love from military action. But "In Between" days, waiting days can be filled with fear, worry, uncertainty, and questions. Sometimes those in between days, those waiting days are the hardest to pass through. I recall a few occasions when I thought those waiting days were the hardest. First, I remember waiting for the news that I was accepted into the AFROTC-UNO program to go to college and get my commission as an officer in the USAF. I was excited to get the news about being accepted to attend UNO.

I also remember applying for a job and going to the interview and feeling good about the interview. But you never know how you really did on the interview until you get that phone call offering you the job or getting the letter in the mail. That's why, when I did interviews these days, I got back with the applicants as soon as possible to let them know one way or the other.

The hardest time for me was the waiting period, especially at my mother's bedside before she passed away.

Patience – "Genius is nothing but a great aptitude for patience."

The trouble with life right now is that it does not always work out in a way that we would like. We cannot always enjoy life – sometimes we must patiently endure it.

In any case, it does no good to complain. Impatience does not take away suffering, it only makes it worse. Of course, to patiently endure the evils of life does not mean that we should ignore them. Sometimes we do precisely that. We avoid going to the doctor, knowing that we have an addiction to drugs or alcohol. We ignore the only source and that is total abstinence.

How much risk and inconvenience do we patiently endure for the sake of wealth? How much time do we spend waiting patiently in line to get that great buy on Black Friday - the day after Thanksgiving - for that popular game or toy?

When I was a young boy, I was not a patient person. Do you think you were patient when you were young? Just think about Christmastime – how patient were you waiting for those Christmas presents? If I had the idea, I acted on it. If a gift was coming, I wanted it then and there. I couldn't possibly see into the future when I could do all the things I wanted to do – meet the perfect girl, graduate from high school, go to college, and start a career and family.

But time and faith have shown me over and over that our job is to be patient, to get up every day and pay attention, watching for the directional signs and who God puts into our lives – never take it lightly. Inherent in this idea of patience is the idea of trust. We have to trust that God is present in our lives, caring and moving and working in us and through us. God is there, pointing the way and whispering suggestions if we are quiet and still enough to notice.

I once saw a banner that read "Please be patient; God isn't finished with me yet." What this really means to me is that we all are being worked on daily. No one is perfectly done or finished. There is always room for improvement.

(Excerpt from the St. Peter Catholic Church bulletin
December 8, 2013)

I am not in a hurry...

I probably should begin with a prayer but I don't. Well at least not that often, except when taking big trips. I have taken a different approach. I now have my own mantra. Like the prayer I don't always say it but in those hectic, frantic moments I recite it. I say it aloud so I can hear myself. It works, too. It changes my behavior, lowers my blood pressure and alters my disposition. It is just one simple phrase that works wonders. It is simply this "I am not in a hurry." Doesn't seem like much but it is quite effective. I buckle my seatbelt and before I turn on the radio I announce it "I'm not in a hurry." It's sort of like that old Seinfeld episode with George's father shouting "Serenity Now." I repeat it again so it sinks in, "I am not in a hurry." How often when I am running late I have the urge to rush, hurry and scramble. No good. I found myself darting out into traffic when I should have waited. I dash through a yellow light or was it red hoping to save a minute or two. I keep my foot on the gas pedal a little bit too long and a little bit too strong. No more. "I am not in a hurry." If I am late so be it, but I arrive more relaxed and in a better disposition.

> *Life is short but it doesn't mean we have to rush through it. Trite but true, take one day at a time. Tomorrow will be here soon enough. Too often I find myself living in the future preoccupied about what might happen and forgetting to live right now. Now there is nothing wrong in planning or looking forward to some future event as long as it doesn't rob you of the now. Having balance helps. Take it slow and appreciate the grace of the moment. On this journey called life remind yourself, "I am not in a hurry" and enjoy the trip.*

Patience is not the ability to wait, but how you act while you are waiting.

Now take 5 minutes and read Proverbs 29.

Don't read another chapter until you write one thing you have learned from your readings today that will help you become a better person.

_____
_____
_____
_____
_____
_____
_____
_____
_____
_____
_____
_____
_____
_____

_____

_____

_____

_____

_____

_____

_____

_____

_____

_____

_____

_____

_____

_____

_____

_____

_____

_____

_____

_____

_____

_____

_____

_____

_____

_____

Proverbs 29:22 – An ill-tempered man stirs up disputes, and a hot headed man is the cause of many sins.

DAY 30 - DETERMINATION/PERSEVERANCE

Hebrews 10:36 - You need to persevere so that when you have done the will of God, you will receive what he has promised.

"Football is life, it requires perseverance, self-denial, hard work, sacrifices, dedication, and respect for authority."
Vince Lombardi

We must control ourselves and we must endure. The fact of the matter is that the longer we live the more ways perseverance will be needed. I fail over and over to succeed. Get over your failures and move on to succeed.

At some point, we all face mountains in life, situations that seem beyond our coping abilities. I've had many mountains to climb in my life, but somewhere not much more than a hill, others seemingly insurmountable with a lot of peaks and valleys. But when you treat them as mere speed bumps in life and choose to go over them slowly and cautiously then the situation you are in seems easier to cope with.

I have always felt that "climbing a mountain" is a fitting analogy for the story of our lives. Most of us want to find that easy mountain to climb and think we have made it to the top. The only mountain we have to climb in this life is the mountain of our daily tasks, a mountain that promises not glory but only frustration. All our burdens are like rocks on the side of the mountain and we try to push them up the mountain only to have them roll back down to the bottom of the mountain at the end of the day - waiting for us to begin our struggles again the next morning. Certainly, our life on an ordinary day has its fair share of suffering and depending on which path we take or which decision we make, has a bearing on the outcome. We are going to have obstacles along our way as we climb the mountain of life. Sometimes they are big boulders and sometimes they are little rocks. Our task is to "climb up" and over the big boulders and to move the little rocks with the right decisions. Our desire for perfect happiness is in fact a desire we all should share. The journey will not always be easy. You may have successfully cleared the path to the top of the mountain, but you still have not arrived at your destination. We are all familiar with the distortions which arise when something is taken out of its context. It can be especially annoying when something we said is quoted back to us in such a way as to miss completely what we meant and what we said.

> The challenge is to accept the life that has been given to us.

Persevere: What you are is what you will be and all you can do is to have the courage to accept the fact and make the best of what you have. We need the bravery to look honestly at ourselves and identify our true strengths and true weaknesses. To some extent the abilities we have can point to the way of life we should choose. Finally, we need the bravery to *persevere* in a life which is probably the right one, but in the beginning, it is going to seem to be a burden. We may be suddenly overcome by a feeling that our lives have been wasted, that we have been spinning our wheels in cars mired in mud. We say to ourselves: "There must be something better in life than this! There must be another way of life that is easier, more fruitful, more meaningful, and more important. This challenge to accept the life that has been given us calls for the greatest courage.

None of us would have survived our early years without the trust we had in our parents when they told us something. We are cracked and weak. We don't always know where we are going or what we are to do. Still, there is no reason for despair.

On November 1, 2014, my niece, Robin was run over in a parking lot and was in critical condition – a coma -- for 30 days. Surgery was performed to remove part of her skull to relieve the pressure on her brain. Miraculously it relieved the pressure and she started to recover 60 days after the accident. She started her **long** rehab. She has a great sense of humor and strong perseverance. She has surprised the doctors and her family with her recovery and is on the road to full recovery and she is a walking miracle to say the least.

"Patience and perseverance have a magical effect before which difficulties disappear and obstacle vanishes."
John Quincy Adams

"Do what you can, with what you have, where you are."
Theodore Roosevelt

"Our desire to excel helps us to exceed our expectations!"
Unknown source

Determination/Perseverance,
The Last Game is about Freddie Steinmark.
Excerpt from Ricki Taylor's Motivational Moment.

Despite being chosen to receive the Golden Helmet Award from the Denver Post as the best high school football player in the state of Colorado, Freddie Steinmark went unnoticed by colleges. His 5'9" 150lb body just didn't fit the "profile" of what even the smaller colleges wanted. That changed when Coach Darrell Royal of the University of Texas (UT) saw film on the diminutive player and decided to take a chance. He sent one of his assistant coaches, Fred Akers to Steinmark's hometown of Wheat Ridge, Colorado. Akers rang the doorbell of the Steinmark residence and thought the young man who answered the door must be Freddie's little brother. The high school athlete was invited on an official visit to the Texas campus. He wore boots with high heels hoping to look taller on his visit.

Coach Royal met with the young athlete from Colorado and Freddie was shocked by what the coach told him. "Son let me tell you something very interesting," Royal said. "I didn't get to the University of Oklahoma until I was 25 years old because of the war. I was just about your size. I quarterbacked the Oklahoma Sooners to a national championship one year. On defense, I broke the record for interceptions. I don't care how big you are."

That day Steinmark committed to UT and made a vow to himself that he would start every game. He did not care how high the odds were stacked. When Steinmark arrived for fall practice, sophomore rover Mike Campbell mistook him for a team manager.

"The kid looked like he was 15 years old," Campbell recalled.

That was before Steinmark was issued a uniform and began knocking freshman teammates all over the field. In 1967 freshman football players could not play varsity but Freddie made his mark on the freshman team leading in interceptions and a 76-yard punt return against Texas A&M.

At the very start of his sophomore year he replaced the starting safety and fulfilled his dream of making first string for the

Longhorns. He was making good grades, attending college with his high school sweetheart and never missed mass at his church.

The season started out slow with a tie and a loss but after James Street became the starting quarterback in the Texas wishbone offense, they produced eight straight wins, a Cotton Bowl victory over Tennessee and ranked third in the nation.

The 1969 season began with great promise for the Longhorns and Freddie Steinmark was a preseason All Southwest Conference selection at safety. Over that summer before the 1969 season the owner of the dealership where he worked noticed Freddie limping. When he arrived on campus it was evident to the coaches that something was wrong. Despite the limp he performed on the field and Texas breezed through the season with nine wins.

The limp got worse during the season and the Texas coaching staff considered benching Steinmark but after much thought they felt his contribution to the team's 18 game winning streak earned him a second chance and he came through never getting beat deep and remained the most devastating hitter on the team.

The final game of the season was against Arkansas with Texas ranked number one in the nation and Arkansas number two. Freddie Steinmark played like a champion with Texas winning in the last minutes of the game. One of the players noticed after the game that Freddie was crying, but it was not from being overjoyed, it was from the tremendous pain in his leg.

Three days later he confessed to Coach Royal that he had trouble walking. He was sent to Houston's M.D. Andersen Hospital for x-rays and they discovered an abnormal growth in his left thighbone. After a biopsy was performed it was confirmed that over an inch of his femur was devoured by cancer. Emergency surgery was performed to amputate his left leg at the hip.

Within a few days he was up and walking on crutches and vowed that he would be on the sidelines in nineteen days when Texas played Notre Dame in the Cotton Bowl. When he came out of the tunnel at the game he received a standing ovation from the entire stadium. Twelve days later, he walked across the stage at the athletic banquet on a shiny new prosthetic to receive his letter jacket from Royal. There was not a dry eye among the 6,000 fans at the Austin Municipal Auditorium.

He never gave up, he learned how to drive a car with one leg, water ski, and learned to play golf. He asked his high school sweetheart to marry him and she accepted. The wedding day was never to be, the cancer had spread and in May of 1971 Freddie Steinmark left this world. His funeral in Denver, Colorado is said to be the largest crowd in the history of the state.

When players run through the tunnel before home games at Texas there are two large photographs of Freddie Steinmark. Each player touches a picture and gives the "hook 'em horns" sign as a tribute to a young man they have never met but remains an inspiration to this day.

What Freddie Steinmark taught was not about dying with dignity, it was a roadmap on how to live life to the fullest with no excuses and with full effort. Even in the worst of circumstances Freddie Steinmark took full responsibility for how he lived his life. As each day unfolds let it be your best day, that's what Freddie would have done.

"Destiny is not a matter of chance; it is a matter of choice. It is not a thing to be waited for. It is a thing to be achieved."
William Jennings Bryant

Now take 5 minutes and read Proverbs 30.

Don't read another chapter until you write one thing you have learned from your readings today that will help you become a better person.

_____

_____

_____

_____

_____

_____

Proverbs 30:5 - *Every word of God is tested; he is a shield to those who take refuge in him.*

DAY 31 - NEVER, NEVER QUIT!

Philippians 4:13 - I can do all things through Christ who strengthens me.

Winston Churchill is best known for his saying:
"Never, never quit."

The first key victory you must win is over yourself. Your chief competition is you! How many times have you started something, like running, losing weight, praying, working out, or any one of your New Year's resolutions? I remember when I was going to college and I started a running program to stay in shape. People told me that it would not last. Well, it lasted for 20 years. I ran marathons (26.2 miles), half marathons (13.1 miles), 10k (6.2 miles), and 5k (3.1miles) races. I failed over and over before I managed to succeed. I wanted to run the races at an average 6-minute pace for the race, and I kept on working hard to achieve that goal. I had to get over my failures and move on in order to succeed. Finally, my work paid off, and I started running the 5k and 10k races under a 6-minute pace, and I eventually ran a half marathon under a 6-minute pace for the entire race.

You're going to fall down, but the world doesn't care how many times you fall down, as long as it's one fewer than the number of times you get back up.

Everyone around you has a story to tell! And you have a story to tell also.

Having survived the perils of "growing up," we began the flourishing days of our youth, and our expectations grew even larger. After all we were young, naïve, and strong. The future seemed to be in our hands. We thought we could make ourselves anything we wanted to be. We looked forward to becoming a success, finding people who would like us, or at least respect us, hoping that we would find someone somewhere who would love us, be friends with us, perhaps even share their life with us. Of course, our expectations were not without fear. We knew that life was not perfect, that it was possible to fail, that it was possible to love and not be loved. Most of life only exists in memories.

> The only way we can lose is to quit.

Amazingly, sometimes what you think is your greatest weakness can become a wonderful strength.

The only way we can lose is to quit.

We may never achieve perfection, but we can keep asking our Father for His help.

I want to tell you a couple of stories about never quitting. I was watching the movie "Tin Cup" about a golfer. The golfer was Roy McAvoy played by Kevin Costner. Roy McAvoy was a burned out, washed out, down-n-out golfer who earned his way into the US Open Golf Tournament. A PGA Golf Tournament is 72 holes of golf over 4 days. Roy McAvoy was leading the US Open going to the 72nd hole. The last hole was a par 5 meaning that it took 5 shots to get the ball into the hole without losing any strokes. Roy McAvoy hit a great drive and then took out a 3 wood to hit the ball over water and land it on the green. This would give him a 3 or 4 and win the tournament. Unfortunately, his first shot with the 3-wood hit the green, but the ball rolled back and into the water. He had the choice to move up closer to hit his next shot, but he refused. He wanted to show everyone that he could put it on the green from that spot with a 3 wood, but every try the ball kept going into the water. This is until he hit his 12th shot. That's when the ball hit the green and went into the hole. The point is that Roy McAvoy would not give up until he made it over the water and the ball stayed on the green.

Do you remember reading the story about "The Little Engine That Could" by Walter Pipe? The story was about a little red train that carried all kinds of toys and food to boys and girls over a mountain. But, one time the little red engine tried to get over the mountain and it broke down. Different engines came by the little red engine, but none would help until the little blue engine decided to help the broken-down red engine. The little blue engine had never been over the mountain. The little blue engine hooked up to the red engine and train. The little blue engine went choo choo, I think I can, I think I can, I know I can, I know I can, I think I can, I think I can, I know I can. Up, up, up, faster and faster and faster and faster the little blue engine climbed up the mountain until at last it reached the top of the mountain and the train started going down the other side. The point is that the little blue engine never, never quit.

"If"
by Rudyard Kipling

If you can keep your head when all about you,
Are losing theirs and blaming it on you,
If you can trust yourself when all men doubt you,
But make allowance for their doubting too;
If you can wait and not be tired by waiting,
Or being lied about, don't deal in lies,
Or being hated, don't give way to hating,
And yet don't look too good, nor talk too wise:

If you can dream—and not make dreams your master;
If you can think—and not make thoughts your aim;
If you can meet with Triumph and Disaster
And treat those two impostors just the same;
If you can bear to hear the truth you've spoken
Twisted by knaves to make a trap for fools,
Or watch the things you gave your life to, broken,
And stoop and build 'em up with worn-out tools:
If you can make one heap of all your winnings
And risk it on one turn of pitch-and-toss,
And lose, and start again at your beginnings
And never breathe a word about your loss;
If you can force your heart and nerve and sinew
To serve your turn long after they are gone,
And so hold on when there is nothing in you
Except the Will which says to them: 'Hold on!'
If you can talk with crowds and keep your virtue,
Or walk with Kings—nor lose the common touch,
If neither foes nor loving friends can hurt you,
If all men count with you, but none too much;
If you can fill the unforgiving minute
With sixty seconds' worth of distance run,
Yours is the Earth and everything that's in it,
And—which is more—you'll be a Man, my son!

Success in life comes when you simply refuse to give up, with
goals so strong that obstacles, failures,
and loss only act as motivation.

You have to love what you do to be successful.
Never, Never Give Up!

Now take 5 minutes and read Proverbs 31.

Don't read another chapter until you write one thing you have learned from your readings today that will help you become a better person.

_____

_____

_____

_____

_____

_____

_____

_____

_____

_____

_____

_____

_____

_____

_____

_____

_____

_____

_____

_____

_____

_____

_____

_____

_____

_____

_____

Proverbs 31:31 - Give her a reward of her labors,
and let her works praise her at the city gates.

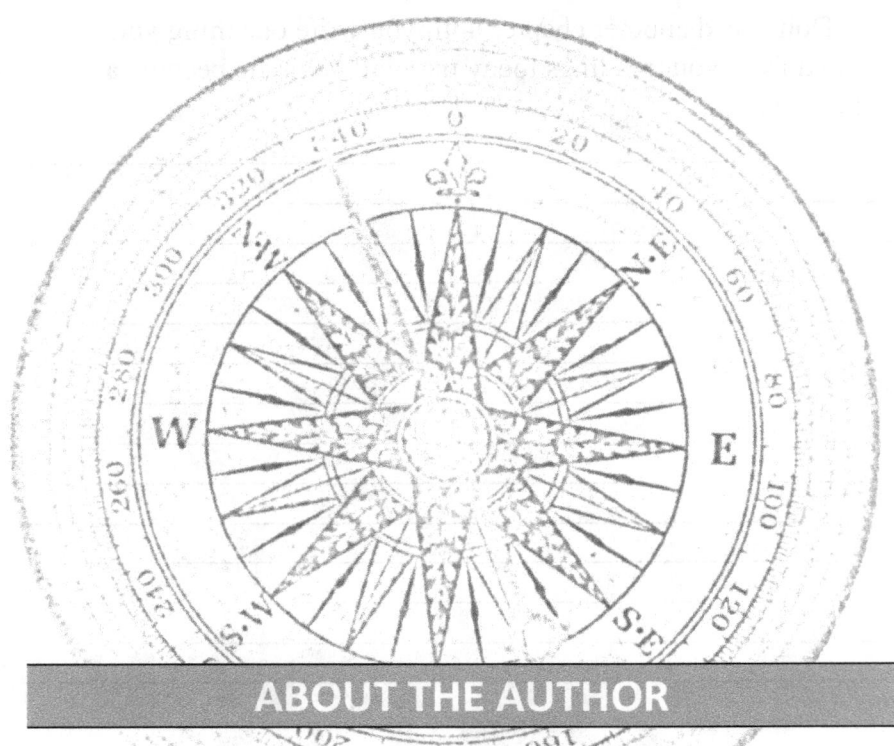

ABOUT THE AUTHOR

Russell Wetherington enjoys inspiring others to have a positive attitude with high ethical and moral values. Since a young child, he has been in some kind of leadership role from a newspaper boy in his early teens, a manager of a gas station in high school, and as a young Sergeant in the Air Force where he was in charge of the golf course maintenance for the base golf course.

In 1978 Russell earned a Bachelor of General Studies from the University of Nebraska at Omaha in Omaha, Nebraska. He also earned the recognition as a distinguished graduate from the Air Force Reserve Officer Training Corp. (ROTC), and was commissioned an Officer in the Air Force and returned to active duty and served for twenty-one years in many leadership roles and organizations.

When he retired from the Air Force, he started another career in public government, progressing from a purchasing agent to the position as the Assistant County Administrator - General Services for

Hernando County, Florida. While in public government he has held numerous management positions and has been responsible for training Commissioners and key management personnel. As a high achiever in management and leadership he has been sought by other managers to share how he stays so positive and his knowledge on team building skills.

Russell Wetherington believes that WHO ARE YOU? is a book that relates to all those people who were told that they could not do anything or amount to anything in life. The Author saw quite clearly that, if you had a positive attitude and were willing to listen and work hard, you could be successful. He believes that each of us has what it takes to be successful and the 31 chapters in 31 days can truly help make you "Who You Are."

With my Mom & brothers at a seafood restaurant for her birthday.
She loved seafood for her birthday!
Cliff, Jack, Wayne, Mom, me, & George.